From CHAOS to Calm

From CHAOS to Calm

The Power, Purpose, and
Promise of Solution-Focused
Communication

Bill Crawford, Ph.D.

Florence Publishing
Houston, Texas

Manufactured in the United States of America
Library of Congress Catalog Card Number: 99-095095
ISBN: 0-9653461-1-0
Text graphics: Created by Bill Crawford
Cover illustrations and graphics: Steve Butler, Bill Crawford, Robert Smith, and Tim Teebken of Artville, L.L.C. - Additional illustrations: Dover Publications, Inc.

Bill Crawford, Ph.D.
6750 West Loop South, Ste. 500
Bellaire, Texas 77401
1-888-530-8550
Web site - billcphd.com
Email billcphd@aol.com

To Georgia,
Christopher, &
Nicholas
with all my love

Acknowledgments

Each time I attempt a project as all-encompassing as writing a book, I am reminded of how much the talents and contributions of others play an integral part in creating the final product. I am grateful for the opportunity to thank these individuals and organizations for their support.

Let me begin close to home and start by thanking my wife Georgia, for her support, patience, and enthusiasm for this project. Not only did she spend many a sleepless night proofing and making changes in the final manuscript, she did this while continuing her multi-generational role as loving mother to our two sons, Christopher and Nicholas, and loving daughter to her father and mother, Dr. and Mrs. Socrates Rombakis. I am continually amazed at how having her as a relationship partner has enriched my life and allowed me to do the work that I do from a foundation of love. Further, not only has she been a significant factor in the creation of this foundation, she continues to be an example of the power of love as a resource for re-creating a sense of family on a daily basis.

Let me also thank my two sons, Christopher and

Nicholas (ages 8 and 4) for understanding when I was away and yet, never letting me get away without a hug. They continue to be a reminder of the boundless energy and joy of childhood and the power of imagination. This book, as well as, everything else I do, is dedicated to Georgia, Christopher, and Nicholas, with all my love.

Further in the spirit of acknowledging family, let me thank my father-in-law and mother-in-law, Dr. and Mrs. Socrates Rombakis. They are especially important to me given that my own mother and father passed away when I was in my early twenties. As with Georgia, they are always there with a supportive word and willingness to help in any way. In addition, they continue to show our two sons what a gift it is to have a loving "YiaYia" and "Papou" (grandmother and grandfather) as part of one's family. Special thanks to my mother-in-law, Effie Rombakis, who spent countless hours proofing the manuscript.

Also I would like to thank my brother-in-law Andrew Rombakis M.D., for his excellent proofing and editing suggestions. His willingness to take the time to read the book from his unique, objective perspective has improved the quality of the message immeasurably. Further, I would like to thank my aunt, Mrs. Dorothea Husson, for devoting an extensive amout of her Texas vacation to proofreading the manuscript. As you can see, bringing this book to its final form has truly been a "family affair".

Next, I would like to thank one of my closest friends, Steve Butler for his work on the cover (he created the flames on "Chaos", as well as, many other creative touches). His expertise in graphic design has greatly enhanced the look of the book, as his friendship continues to enhance my life. His consistent genuineness, humor, creativity and quality of character make him a joy to work with, and my hope is that someday (soon) we will turn our friendship into a business partnership.

Sometimes you need a reason to write a book (or at least I do). Each of the two books I have written so far have been created as a result of PBS specials produced here in Houston at the local PBS affiliate, KUHT. Therefore, I would like to thank the station manager, John Hesse, the program director, Ken Lawrence, and the general manager and CEO Jeff Clarke, for their ongoing support in the production of this second PBS special and resulting book. Further, I would like to thank Robert Smith for the creation of the "conflict collage" that he has allowed me to use as a background for the cover of the book, as well as, many of the graphics during the special.

Again, because the creation of the PBS special played such an integral part in the creation of this book, I would like to thank all of the people associated with this project: Jeffrey Weiss, Mike Looper, John Hesse, F. Christian Boyd, Steve Pyndus, Joe Brueggeman, John Ahrens, Brad Burkons, Robert Smith, Lorinda Boyd, Brad Burkons, Ben Cowpersmith, Shannon Harrison, L. Kirk Kauder, Eric Wall, Ray Gutierrez, Fujio Watanabe, Doug Robertson, Frank Castro, Matt Brawley, Doug Mueller, Ainsworth Duvernay, Phillip Williams, Ozzie Ausburne, Jim Koehn, Joan Havis, Steve Butler, Leslie Norman, Josue Maymi, Linda Garrett, and Georgia Crawford.

One of the individuals mentioned above that disserves a special thanks is my producer/director Jeff Weiss. His attention to detail, talent, and candid suggestions from the original discussions to the final edit were crucial in bringing this project to fruition. This is the second project of this nature that I have had the pleasure to work with Jeff and he continues to impress me with his knowledge of the process, from an artistic, logistical, and interpersonal perspective.

I would also like to thank Tom Blackwell and Mark Basile of First American Financial. It was their enthusiasm for, and belief in the value of this material that initiated the discussions which resulted in both the PBS Special and this book. It's such a pleasure to work with individuals such as Mark and Tom and organizations such as First American Financial, who so clearly value people, as well as, the bottom line.

And finally, I would like to thank my mother and father, Florence and Burton Crawford. Even though they passed away almost 26 years ago, I am touched daily by their warmth, love, and philosophy of life. Their commitment to creating a loving home for me, as well as, helping others through the programs of A.A. and Alanon has given me a foundation on which to build a life and a life's work. In many ways, they live on in every word of this book.

Contents

From CHAOS to Calm

Part I

The Problem

Chapter 1

Riding the Cycle of Conflict

*R*ude, demanding, pushy, deceitful, arrogant, loud, obnoxious, manipulative, intimidating, insulting... have you noticed how disruptive certain types of people can be in our lives? One run-in with these difficult people and what was previously a good day can become a stressful experience that seems to grow more and more frustrating. Further, this anxiety-laden interaction can color our experience of everything (and everyone) we encounter, which only serves to create more stress and anxiety. Truth is, whether we are talking about family or strangers, in-laws or outlaws, babies or bosses, the known or the unknown, dealing with difficult people can be one of life's most "difficult" experiences, and one that seems to pop up in our lives all too often. In fact, as a speaker and corporate trainer, conflict resolution (or dealing with difficult people) is one of my most frequently-requested seminars.

My goal in writing this book, therefore, is to give you the tools to understand and deal more effectively with these conflicted situations. In order to do this, we are going to look at conflict from three perspectives:

1. What are the underlying causes of conflict, and how can a simple disagreement turn into a vicious cycle that seems to feed off of itself?

2. When we find ourselves dealing with a difficult person or caught in a conflict, how can we interact with this person in a way that not only diffuses the conflict, but actually taps into their internal motivation to hear what we say as valuable?

3. How can we stop conflict before it starts, or how can we deal with people so that we find ourselves in fewer and fewer conflicts in the first place, without sweeping the problems under the rug?

By the way, the reason we are focusing on "difficult" people is because I am going to assume that most of us are pretty good at dealing with "normal" people, or those individuals who are willing to sit down and have a normal conversation and/or deal with a disagreement in a calm, rational manner. If you are like most folks, it's those "difficult" people that seem to get under your skin.

Let's start by getting a mental picture of just exactly "who" we are talking about. One way to do this is to think of the adjectives that you would use to describe the difficult people you have encountered. Now, these may not be the adjectives that you would *say to their face*, but way deep down in the pit of your stomach, when you are dealing with these folks, what are you thinking about them? Well, if you are like most people you probably think of "them" as "rude, obnoxious, loud, arrogant, demanding, rigid, crazy, etc.

By the way, it's probably fair to say that we could fill several pages with these adjectives, so why don't we just let this list represent all the ways we find ourselves thinking about difficult people? In other words, if your adjectives (or the way you might describe a difficult person) aren't on the list, just imagine that they are, and we can move on   Now, have you noticed that when we are dealing with people like this we tend to react in certain ways? These may not be the ways we think we necessarily "should" react, but way down deep inside, in the pit of our stomach, when we are dealing with these "rude, obnoxious, loud, arrogant" people, how do we find ourselves reacting?

Isn't it true that we can also find *ourselves* becoming defensive, frustrated (have you noticed how frustrating it is to deal with these people?!!), angry, and loud (in fact, we often try to get our point across by just becoming louder than "them"!)? In addition, some of us respond by becoming withdrawn. In other words, the response can take on a fight-or-flight characteristic. We may also respond by feeling superior or confused, wondering, "Why are you treating me this way, I haven't done anything to you? In fact, I'm trying to give you important information!" By the way, we could probably fill several pages with adjectives describing our reaction as well, so why don't we just let these represent how we tend to respond to "them". Needless to say, dealing with difficult people can be a very stressful experience.

Now, here's something very, very important. . . . we all know that "they" are the difficult people . . . and "we" are the nice people! Why would I say that they are the difficult people and we are the nice people, when it looks like we are doing some of the *same things*?!?! . . . Because, . . . THEY STARTED IT!!!!!!! Right? We were just doing our job, and minding our own business when they came along being "rude, obnoxious, loud, arrogant, demanding, rigid, crazy", and we responded by becoming "defensive, frustrated, loud, withdrawn," etc.

Them!	Us!
Rude	Defensive
Obnoxious	Frustrated
Loud	Loud
Arrogant	Withdrawn
Demanding	Superior
Rigid	Confused
Crazy	Crazy

This would be bad enough (stressful, frustrating) if it stopped there, but have you noticed that it doesn't? In fact, when they are being "rude, obnoxious, loud, etc., and we respond by becoming "defensive, frustrated, superior," etc., what do they do, or how do they respond to our response? Yes, they become even *more* "rude, demanding, rigid, crazy" (or more difficult) to which we respond by becoming even *more* stressed, frustrated, angry, insistent, sarcastic, demanding, pushy, loud, intimidating, etc. etc.

Of course by this time, they are seeing *us* as the difficult person and they believe that they're reacting to *us*, while we, of course, see *them* as the difficult person, and think we are reacting to *them*, and a reaction cycle of them to us, and us to them, them/us, us/them, them/us, builds until something explodes!

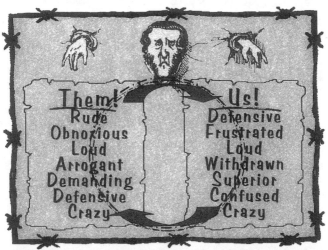

THE CYCLE OF CONFLICT

I call this ever-escalating tendency for us to react to them while they are reacting to us the *Cycle of Conflict!* Does this "Us versus Them" cycle feel familiar to you? That is, have you ever found yourself in a conflict where "they" are seeing you and your reaction as part of the problem, and becoming more difficult? If so, welcome to the human race! The fact is that *almost everybody on the planet reacts this way* (which explains why so many disagreements become destructive conflicts.) Let's examine this cycle further and see what sort of problems it could cause. In other words, what do you think would happen if this cycle came to represent our relationship with this person? Well, first, nothing would get accomplished because there would be no communication. Right?

When both parties are using all their energy just reacting to each other, there is no room, or even desire for true communication or productivity. That is, if we really needed them to listen to us or if we needed information from them, chances are that neither would happen.

Second, because "they" see "*us*" as the difficult person, they are likely to go tell someone, or find someone to complain to, and we all know how destructive gossip or negative word of mouth can be to the success of almost any group of people, from a family to an organization. Third, we become *All Stressed Up & Nowhere To Go!* (Which, aside from this being a wonderfully descriptive phrase, it also happens to be the title of my first book).

Have you ever noticed how stressful dealing with one of these people can be? We can be having a perfectly normal day, no real problems, and one of "these" people comes into our lives seeming to vibrate with their "difficult" energy, and pretty soon, we seem to have caught it! Further, even when they leave, we continue to feel resentful! There is a great quote that speaks to this, how resentment can affect our experience of life and it says:

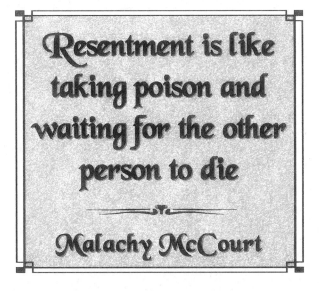

Resentment is like taking poison and waiting for the other person to die

Malachy McCourt

Isn't that the truth? Often, "they" will have no idea that we're upset, and yet the "poison" can eat at us for hours, days, or even weeks! Further, this "poison" can then affect the way we interact with others. For example, after we have dealt with this difficult person, and someone else comes in to ask us a question, because we are still "infected" with the stress and frustration of the last interaction, we might find ourselves saying, "What do you want?#&!@&*!!," or responding in some other negative way. In other words, we often take this frustration out on the next person we encounter, or even worse, we save it up and take it home, where we take it out on our family! So clearly, we must do something about this problem, but what?

Frequently, our first tendency in a disagreement, especially one that has become problematic, is to look for who is to blame, again, "who started it?", or who's "right" and, who's "wrong." The belief here is that if they are wrong, then *they* are responsible for the problem, and they must be the one to apologize and/or change. However, if *we* are wrong, then *we* must be the one to change. The problem with this perspective is that it rarely solves the problem. In fact, it is often one of the main factors in the escalation of the disagreement. Remember, we see *them* as the difficult person, and believe that they are causing our reaction (anger, frustration, annoyance, etc.) and they, of course, see *us* as the difficult person and believe that *we* are the problem, and the cycle goes on and on. In fact, you will often hear people who are involved in a conflict say something like, "Me? Why should I have to change (apologize, make the first move, etc.)? *They* are the ones who (started it, said, or did something they shouldn't have, etc., etc.)"

Based on this belief that they are wrong, we try to get them to change. We believe that, "If (fill in the blank) would just stop (blanking), then everything would be fine." Have you noticed, however, that when we try to get them to change, they don't say "Thank you for sharing?" In fact, don't they seem to get worse?

Let me demonstrate this in another way. Try this exercise. Make a fist (or imagine that you have made a fist) as tight as you can. Now, if someone tried to force your fist open, what would be your initial reaction? If you're like most of us, the first thing you would do would be to tighten your grip, or become more resistant to being changed. Guess what... so do they! In other words, *whenever we try to force someone to change, what we are really doing is motivating them to resist us even more!* I call this *The Lesson of the Fist*, and it may be the most important lesson you will learn in dealing with difficult people.

The Lesson of the Fist

Whenever we try to force any one to change, they either resist us, or resent us, or both, & as a result become more motivated to defend their position!

The reason I believe that this lesson is so important is that it addresses why so many of our attempts to solve the problem (or deal with difficult people) fail. They fail because we are still trying to deal with the problem the way we have always tried to deal with the problem, by trying to change the difficult person, and most people react to this attempt to change them by becoming *more resistant.* There is a quote from Albert Einstein that I believe is very applicable here, and that is:

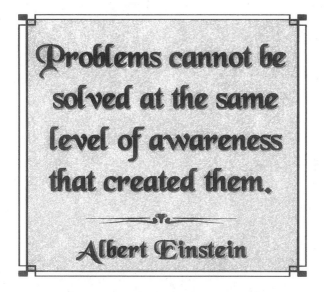

Problems cannot be solved at the same level of awareness that created them.

Albert Einstein

If your goal is to become *more* effective in your interactions with difficult people, meaning have more influence in how they affect you (and how you affect them) then you must start by raising your awareness, or your understanding of what's going on here, or what is truly driving the *Cycle of Conflict.*

You see, most people think that it is the "facts" or what actually happens to us that cause us to experience life (feel, think, behave) the way we do.

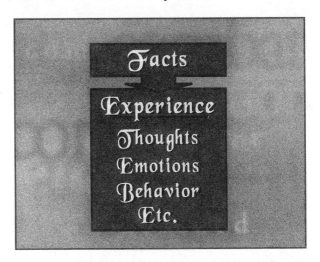

I'm going to suggest that, while the facts do play a role in our experience, they are *not* the main determinant. In fact, I'm going to suggest that the facts are filtered through our beliefs, and it is these *beliefs* that actually determine how we think, feel, and behave.

Let me give you an example of this powerful effect. We all know that there was a time in the evolution of our species when most of the people on the planet believed that the world was flat. Now, of course, the fact was that the earth was round, however, most people firmly believed that the earth was flat. Given that they believed the world was flat, when a ship sailed out to sea and didn't return, what did they think? It must have fallen off the edge, right? You see? Their beliefs (about the world being flat) created their *interpretations*, or gave meaning to what they saw, and these interpretations were often more congruent with their beliefs than the facts.

This tendency for our interpretations to be guided by our beliefs (more than the facts) explains why, when you ask ten witnesses to an accident or crime what they saw, you will often get ten very different stories. All saw the same scene (the facts), but they each interpreted what they saw based upon their beliefs (or mental models, or paradigms.) These beliefs are a result of many factors: life experiences, how (and where) they have grown up, what they have been taught about themselves and the world, etc.. Needless to say that each of us will have a slightly different set of beliefs based upon our past teachings and experiences.

Back to our ship analogy. Remember, the belief was that the world was flat, and this was a truism shared by most of the people during the fourteenth century. As we have discussed, based upon this belief, when a ship sailed out and didn't return, most interpreted that to mean that it had fallen off the edge of the world. Further, based upon this interpretation they would expect that if another ship sailed out too far, it too would fall off of the edge. Right? This adds another piece of awareness to the puzzle of why people think, feel, and behave the way they do... the concept of *expectations*, or what they expect to happen in the future.

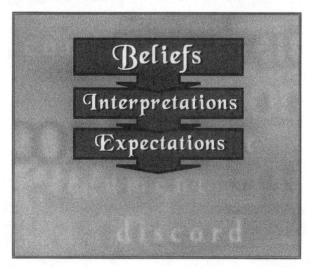

While the degree to which our past affects our present has been the topic of much discussion, the role of our expectations in determining our experience of life has, in my opinion, not been given the emphasis it deserves. For example, let's say that you have had a rotten past, however, for whatever reason you truly believe that your life is going to change for the better. How would you feel right now, at this moment? More congruent with your experience of the past, or your expectations of the future? . . . You see? Our expectations of the future would (and always do) have us thinking, feeling, and doing certain things now, and are therefore, a very powerful component in how we deal with anything in the present.

Let's go back to our "ship" analogy in order to continue to raise our awareness of why people behave the way they do. Remember, the belief was that the world was flat, which led to the interpretation that the ship, which sailed out but didn't return must have fallen off the edge of the earth. This led to the expectation that if another ship sails out too far, it will meet the same fate. Based upon these beliefs, interpretations, and expectations, wouldn't it make sense that most people would have felt frightened, or at least somewhat apprehensive, about sailing on a ship? That's because our beliefs, interpretations, and expectations (which all fall into the category of thoughts), create our emotions. Further, based upon this apprehension, concern, or fear, wouldn't they tend to avoid ships? That's because our *emotions* create our *behaviors*. The end result would be that people avoided ships (or at least those that sailed very far from shore), and believed that they were now safe from falling off the edge of the world because of this decision. This behavior, and resulting positive feeling of safety, then reinforced their original belief that the world is flat.

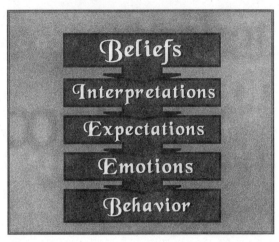

How does this apply to dealing with difficult people? Well, wouldn't it be fair to say that when we encounter a difficult person, we have thoughts such as, "What a jerk!" or "Who do they think they are?" or "They have no right to treat me that way?" Wouldn't it also be fair to say that these thoughts are based upon the belief that they are "wrong" for being "difficult"? (Now remember, I am not trying to suggest that they aren't wrong, I'm just trying to understand the problem so that we can deal with the situation more effectively.) So, we believe that they are wrong for being difficult, which has us interpreting their words and behavior as "bad", "problematic", or at least "unjustified" (Our *beliefs* create our *interpretations*)

Further, based upon these beliefs and interpretations, we probably expect that our interaction with them will continue to be an unpleasant one, and that there is nothing that we can do about it. Based upon these beliefs, interpretations, and expectations about the difficult person, most of us feel some degree of frustration, stress, annoyance, anger, resentment, etc. And then, based upon these emotions we tend to either argue with them, try to convince them to change, complain, tell someone about our experience with them, or just give up.

These emotions and behaviors then become our experience of life with regard to this difficult person, which is added to our experience of what it's like to deal with difficult people in general. This experience then reinforces our "beliefs" about the "fact" that they are wrong and/or have no right to be this way, and the cycle begins again.

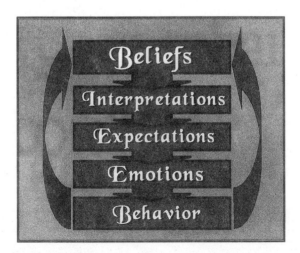

Beliefs

Interpretations

Expectations

Emotions

Behavior

Sound familiar? How's this working for you? I don't mean to be flippant about this subject, for I do know that dealing with conflict can be a very unpleasant experience. I'm just encouraging you to ask a more "purposeful" question, or a question that might be helpful in solving the problem. Rather than, "Who's wrong?", which often only tends to perpetuate the problem, I'm encouraging you, instead, to ask questions that are more likely to lead to solutions, such as, "What is really going on here?" In other words, what are the beliefs that might be driving the difficult person's behavior or, "Why are difficult people being so difficult?"

To answer this question, we must make a distinction between two types of difficult people, the *acute* and the *chronic*. I'm going to suggest that the acutely difficult person is basically a "normal" person who is just having a bad day. At one time or another we have all probably been in this position. Something like a flat tire, argument with a family member, problem at work, etc., has us snapping at people, being disrespectful, or just behaving in ways that are not part of our normal response patterns.

The chronically difficult person, on the other hand, is someone who has been difficult almost all of their lives, and is probably difficult to almost everyone they meet. Since these are the most challenging of the two types, let's look at what's behind their "difficultness", or how their beliefs might affect their behavior. For example, look at the adjectives we have chosen to describe "them" in the *Cycle of Conflict:*

Them!
Rude
Obnoxious
Loud
Arrogant
Demanding
Defensive
Crazy

Us!
Defensive
Frustrated
Loud
Withdrawn
Superior
Confused
Crazy

THE CYCLE OF CONFLICT

What do you think a person like this might believe about the world in general... safe, or unsafe? Unsafe! Absolutely! In fact, they probably think that people are out to get them. What do you think these people believe about the concepts of trust and cooperation? Probably not much. In fact, they may even see these concepts as dangerous. Finally, how do you imagine these people see *themselves*... high or low self-esteem? This can be tricky because they may act as if they hold themselves in high regard. The truth is, however, that this behavior is almost always a cover for a deep sense of insecurity or low self-esteem.

When people have low self-esteem, deep down they believe that something is wrong with them. So, these people think that there is something wrong with them, and guess what? We agree with them, don't we? !!!!!!!!!!!! "Damn straight there's something wrong with you, you #*%@!?#".

Unfortunately, while this perspective is under-standable, it may not be working for us, because in seeing them as "wrong", we may be reinforcing their negative beliefs about themselves and the world. In other words, if the beliefs behind their difficult be-havior are that the world is a dangerous place, people are out to get them, that trust and cooperation are dangerous, and that there is something wrong with them, and we respond to them by becoming defen-sive, annoyed, angry, etc., we may be unintentionally confirming their negative beliefs, and thus *reinforcing the very behavior we want them to change!* It's not "our fault," but it clearly isn't working for us, and we know it!

In other words, if in the middle of one of these encounters we were to stop and ask ourselves, "Is this working for me?" or, "Is how I find myself dealing with this person or situation helping me create the results I want?", most of us would answer, "No". And yet for most of us this tendency to deal with conflict by becoming either offensive or defensive is a famil-iar one, one that we repeat when confronted with such people.

Why do you think this is? In other words, why is it that we find ourselves consistently reacting to difficult people in a way that doesn't serve us? What if we have *learned* to react this way? Let me explain. Remember when you were a child and your parents were being "difficult" with you (angry, annoyed, de-manding, loud, etc.), what did it mean? Didn't it mean

that you were "in trouble" because you had done something wrong? Now, we all know that most of the time
we *had* done something wrong, however that wasn't
the case all the time. Sometimes our parents were just
having a bad day. However, how many of you had
parents that said, "Listen, I'm just having a bad day.
Don't take this personally, it doesn't have anything to
do with you?" Yeah, right!

Same with our teachers! In school, when our
teachers were "difficult" with us (angry, demanding,
annoyed, upset), what did it mean? Again, for most
of us it meant that we had done something wrong,
which again was for the most part, true, but it certainly wasn't *always* true. Sometimes our *teachers* were
just having a bad day! However, how many of you
had the majority of your teachers take responsibility
for their difficult behavior and say, "Listen, I'm just
having a bad day. Don't take this personally?"

Further, this tendency to blame someone else
for one's anger and/or difficult behavior was also
mimicked by our peers. In other words, as children,
when we were dealing with someone who was being
difficult with us, the message was that we had done
something wrong. In fact, we not only got the message that we were wrong, but additionally, that our
parent's, teacher's and/or peer's anger was *our fault*,
or that *we* were the reason they were upset!

Now, when we knew that we *had* done something wrong, that was bad enough. However, do you
remember how it felt when you were being accused
of something that you *knew you didn't do?* Possibly

insulted, righteously indignant, hurt, confused, etc., like they have no right to be upset with me! I didn't do anything wrong! Isn't that somewhat similar to how we feel today when we are dealing with difficult people?

This is what I mean when I suggest that we have learned to react to difficult people the way we do. Most of us grew up being told that when someone was upset with us, it meant something bad about *us*, that *we* had done something wrong and their negative emotion and/or behavior was *our* fault. And this is one of the main reasons we find ourselves becoming so defensive and reactive to difficult people today.

Further, because of this learning, we now not only tend to become defensive (or offensive) when dealing with others, we also tend to blame *them* for *our* anger and difficult behavior. We believe that "they" made us (fill in the blank with "angry", "frustrated", "defensive", etc.). This is another belief that, if left unchallenged, can have a very negative impact on our ability to influence our experience of conflict and/or difficult people.

The good news is that this isn't true, they don't really *make* us feel or do anything. Why is this the good news? Because if they really did have the power to make us feel one thing or another, we would be totally at their mercy, and we would have to change them before we could feel differently. Not only would this give them much more power in our life than we would like, but it would be very frustrating for us! For example, let's look at the *Cycle of Conflict* again.

Them!
Rude
Obnoxious
Loud
Arrogant
Demanding
Defensive
Crazy

Us!
Defensive
Frustrated
Loud
Withdrawn
Superior
Confused
Crazy

THE CYCLE OF CONFLICT

On a scale of 1 to 10, to what degree do you want "them" running your life? Most people would say "Zero!" And yet if we define running our life by occupying our thoughts and emotions, when we react to them with anger, frustration, and rage, to what degree are we *allowing* them to run our lives? See what I mean?

Okay, if others don't make us feel and behave the way we do, what does? Our beliefs, interpretations and expectations! The reason that this is the "good news" is that we have much more influence over our beliefs than we do over other people. Therefore, we have the potential to be very influential in our experience of life.

Still having a hard time with the concept that beliefs have this much power in our lives? Try this example. Let's assume that we are standing in line at a store, waiting to return some defective merchandise, and there are several people in front of us. The clerk is being rude, demanding, pushy, loud, obnoxious, manipulative, intimidating, insulting, sarcastic, arrogant, you know, the typical "difficult" person. As we watch, we become more and more irritated, annoyed, and angry. However, just as we are about to step up and give the clerk a piece of our mind, the person behind us whispers in our ear, "Did you hear that he lost his one-year old daughter in an auto accident a few days ago?" Hmm . . . do we still feel defensive, and frustrated? Are we likely to be loud or feel superior? Look at this... *we are no longer confused.*

THE CYCLE OF CONFLICT

Based upon this new belief, we are now interpreting his behavior in a different light. Based upon this new interpretation, how are we most likely feeling now? Sympathetic, compassionate? Based on these emotions, what is our behavior likely to be?

More patient, understanding, empathic, compassion-ate? In other words, we have moved from confronta-tional to compassionate *without needing "them" to change first.* There is a great quote about the power of compassion to help us deal with our emotions. It says:

Compassion is the antitoxin of the soul: Where there is compassion, even the most poisonous impulses remain relatively harmless.

Eric Hoffer

I really like that first line: "Compassion is the antitoxin of the soul". Remember our discussion about the poisonous effects of resentment? "Resentment is like taking poison and waiting for the other person to die." Well, if resentment is poison (which we can all agree is true) maybe compassion is the antitoxin. . . .

Now, I know that it is hard to have compas-sion for many difficult people, and yet, have you ever had the experience of having a negative reaction to someone only to change that reaction when you learned of the extenuating circumstances? Maybe the

question isn't so much, "Should we be compassionate with difficult people?" Maybe the real question
is, "If we could choose between our "normal" reaction to them and compassion, which would we
choose?"

Let's go back to the "clerk" illustration and
continue to examine the power of beliefs. Now that
someone has told us that the clerk has just lost his
one-year old child, notice what has changed, and what
hasn't. The clerk hasn't changed. He is still being the
same "difficult" person with whom we were originally
annoyed. The only thing that has changed is our beliefs about him and his behavior. "Wait a minute,"
you might say. "It's a different situation now. The
facts have changed." Really? Notice that I didn't say
that we knew for a "fact" that his child had died. Someone just whispered this in our ear. Regardless of the
"facts" (whether or not his child had died), this became a belief about him, and this new belief changed
everything. Instead of seeing him as "disrespectful,
sarcastic, arrogant" we now might interpret his behavior as troubled or overwhelmed. This new interpretation would have us feeling different emotions,
which would have us behaving in a different way.
Basically our entire experience of him and his behavior changed based upon this new belief.

Can you see how this discredits the widely-held
belief that difficult people are responsible for our reactions, that they *make us* angry, annoyed, defensive,
irritated, etc.? The challenge here is not to confuse
"sequence" with "causality." While it's true that our

reactions to them seem to be triggered by their negative behavior, as the "clerk" illustration demonstrates,
our reactions (emotions and behaviors) are *actually* the
result of what we believe about people, and how we
interpret their behavior.

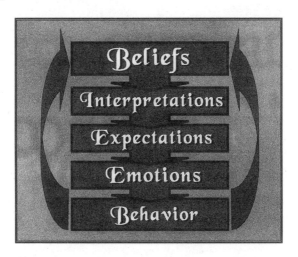

Again, this is the "good news", because if difficult people truly had the power to make us feel and/
or do one thing or another, we would have to change
them before we could feel differently. However, when
we become aware that it is our beliefs about *them* that
are driving our emotions and behaviors, we can
change our reactions (and thus our experience of life
with reference to these types of people) by changing
our beliefs. Granted, this is easier said than done.
However, as I have said before, we have a *lot* more
influence over our beliefs than we do other people.

I want to be clear that when I say it's our beliefs that are causing our reaction, I'm not saying that

it's our "fault" because I don't believe that placing blame solves the problem. In fact, even though I humorously suggested earlier that "they started it", I *really* believe that the need to place blame is a significant part of the problem. Instead of blaming "them", I'm suggesting that we become more aware of what isn't working for us, so that we can move to what does, or become more influential in how we react to the difficult people in our lives (and even how they react to us).

In other words, now that we have raised our awareness of "the problem," let's shift our discussion to the solution. If you happened to notice at the beginning of the book, I managed to sneak in a second subtitle, "The Purpose, Power, and Promise of Solution-Focused Communication". The term "solution-focused" was first coined by Steve DeShazer and Kim Soo Ing from the Milwaukee Brief Family Therapy Training Center. They introduced this term to describe a new approach to helping people change. This new approach focused less on the past (or the problem), and more on potential solutions (hence the term "solution-focused"). I am borrowing this term (with permission) in order to distinguish my approach to dealing with difficult people from other books and trainings on the subject.

You see, I believe that once we have identified what isn't working (the *Cycle of Conflict*), continuing to focus on "the problem" and how bad it is, becomes part of the problem! Instead, I believe that it would be more helpful to focus on what you want to achieve (the solution), and help you become a powerful force in creating this solution. Put another way, this book is not just about "putting out fires" or just resolving conflict, for we all know that even when a fire has been "put out", there are often smoldering embers lying just beneath the surface ready to flare up at a moment's notice.

The purpose of this book is to help you move beyond mere conflict resolution, and actually change your relationship with difficult people so that they begin to see you as an ally versus an enemy. Further, I want to help you become *more* influential in your dealings with others by tapping into their internal motivation to *hear your ideas and suggestions as valuable*. The question, of course, is, "How?"

The first part of that question has been the focus of Part One. So far, we have raised our awareness of the underlying components of conflict, and discovered how a simple disagreement can turn into a vicious cycle of us reacting to them, and them reacting to us. We have examined how, when we try to deal with the conflict from within the cycle by trying to change the other person first, they become more resistant (the Lesson of the Fist). And finally, we have uncovered the *real* cause of their (and our) interpretations, emotions, and behavior... our collective beliefs.

Now, let's move to the second part of the equation, which is, when we find ourselves in conflict or dealing with a "difficult" person, how can we interact with them in a way that not only resolves the conflict, but actually taps into their internal motivation to hear what we say as valuable, creates a solution that they are more likely to support, and again, lays the foundation for a successful working relationship with this person in the future?

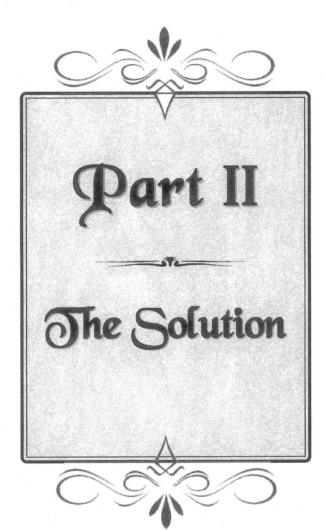

Part II

The Solution

Chapter 2

Active Versus Receptive

*I*n defining the solution, we must first become clear about what we really want to happen, or the results we are trying to create. For example, while we do want others to hear and value what we have to say, there will also be times when we want to be able to get information from them. In other words, isn't it true that what we are really looking to create is effective *two-way* communication, where we can give and receive information in a mutually-beneficial way?

Further, as I have mentioned earlier, rather than just solve the "problem du jour" or the situation of the moment, wouldn't it be more productive to actually build a relationship with this person that allowed you to address and solve problems in the future? In order for this to happen, or, for that matter, in order for communication to go forward in any situation, two "forces" or "energies" must be present: *active* and *receptive*.

Notice, I didn't say active and passive, but active and *receptive*. The problem is that most of us believe the active (the person doing the talking, etc.) is the most powerful. Therefore, we tend to adopt this active position, especially in a conflict. Again, this is a learned tendency, or perspective. All we have to do is think back to when we were children, and ask ourselves whether the powerful people in our lives were generally active or receptive? Active, right? How does this affect our interactions today? Let's look again at the Cycle of Conflict.

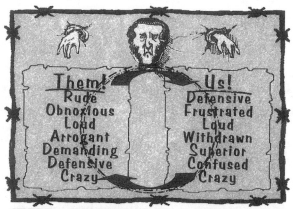

THE CYCLE OF CONFLICT

Would you say that the people in the left-hand column ("them") are more likely to be active or receptive? Most people would say "active". They are being *actively* difficult or resistant. Further, as we have discussed, if we try to be "active" back, we create the other side of the cycle, and the problem gets worse. If you have determined that this doesn't work for you, and you are looking for a more effective way to communicate and/or deal with conflict, let me suggest the often-underestimated "receptive" position. In fact, I'm going to suggest that, in almost all situations, but *especially where conflict or resistance are present*, the receptive role is even *more* powerful that the active.

We see this all the time in the world of martial arts. It's quite common for a skilled practitioner to deflect the blow of a larger, stronger opponent, and send him sprawling using seemingly very little effort. Compare this to the more "traditional" form of combat, where one fighter tries to "win" by being stronger and hitting harder, and the value and power of the receptive role becomes even clearer.

In fact, I'm going to suggest that, even if we could always be assured of "winning" using the active role, the receptive would still be a better choice. Let me explain. Imagine I am a very "powerful" person in an organization, and I wield that power with an iron fist. When I say "jump", people say "how high?", and when someone steps out of line, I make sure that they regret that decision for a long time! I come across a difficult person, immediately move to the active position and, using my strength (intimidation, brow-beating, etc.), *I bring them to their knees, ha, ha!* What do you think is going through the mind of the person I have just "defeated"? Yep. I have just created what I call an "Ambassador of Doom" who now is very motivated to seek some sort of revenge, as well as, tell everyone they know about me and my !%$#@*?! organization.

You see? Even though I've won, I've lost, and this can cost me and my business dearly. In fact, research suggests that when people feel they have been treated with a lack of respect, they will tell up to twelve people (and now with the Internet, they can push a button and tell *twelve thousand* people!). Unfortunately, on the flip side, when people feel they have been treated well, they will only tell about *three* people. It's just human nature. When we feel we have been treated badly, we want to tell someone in order to confirm the righteousness of our position and/or get back at those who "wronged" us by convincing others to not patronize that business. Any way you look at it, by taking the active position, I've lost.

Let's look at how a difficult situation might be handled differently by a person taking the receptive role. In this case, using an analogy from Aikido (one of the most respected forms of martial art) when someone is hurling an insult (or throwing a verbal punch), one doesn't retaliate from an aggressive or "active" position, or even stand there and take it. Instead, one first simply steps out of the way. This is because the goal here is not to stop their punch and hit back harder, but instead, the initial goal is *not to get hit in the first place!* Further, when someone throws a verbal punch, they generally put a lot of energy behind it, expecting that you will counter with your own assault. *This has them off balance!* As you become receptive and step aside, this gives you the opportunity to influence the direction of the interaction by using their energy (or more accurately, blending their energy with yours), and using your combined energies to move the conversation in a direction that you want it to go. In fact, one of the translations of the word "Aikido" is "resolving conflict by blending energies".

Imagine a skilled practitioner of Aikido dealing with a person hurling a verbal insult by adroitly stepping aside, and then rather than throwing the difficult person to the floor, she gently takes his arm and begins to *lead him in the direction that he is already moving.* In one fluid motion, she has transformed herself from the object of his anger to his partner in a journey of discovery, and actually becomes *more* influential in the process because she is using the power of the receptive position and blending it with the active to move toward a solution.

Now, it's important to note here that there are two components of this powerful, receptive position that are absolutely essential to its success: (a) sincerity, and (b) a mutually-beneficial solution. That is, in order for the person who initially threw the verbal punch to follow you, or allow you to lead, or influence the interaction, they must believe that you are *sincerely* interested in their point of view *and* willing to take the conversation in a direction that would be good for all concerned. If you try to manipulate them by just pretending to be interested in their position, they will probably sense this insincerity and resist your influence. (Remember, if they are one of those chronically-difficult people, they already are afraid that the world is out to trick them, or take advantage of them). This doesn't mean that you have to agree with them, or even give in to what they want. It just means that, in dealing with difficult people, we must be willing to move from the active to the receptive position long enough to see their perspective as valuable information, or at least information about what's important to them, and why they are being so difficult.

Another way that I demonstrate this "blending" in my seminars is by holding up two glasses of water, one filled with yellow liquid, and the other blue. I use these colors to represent two sets of opinions, beliefs, or ideas about the situation, ours (blue) and theirs (yellow). My goal in this demonstration is to illustrate that trying to deal with the problem by making them change, would be like trying to *force* them to change their yellow water to blue. Not only would it be impossible, but our insistence would probably only result in them arguing more vehemently for their right to believe what they believe, or holding on to their ideas and refusing to listen to ours.

What if, instead, we didn't start by trying to force them to change, or forcing our ideas upon them, but instead, adopted the powerful receptive position and began to see their ideas (their yellow water) as valuable information, versus just seeing them as "full of it," like we may have done in the past?

Then, we can explore the *second* important

component in resolving conflict, discovering that there are at least five universal reasons why people may be difficult in the first place, and that if we can understand these reasons, we can become more influential in resolving the conflict. Let's look at some of those reasons, and how we can use the receptive position to influence the interaction.

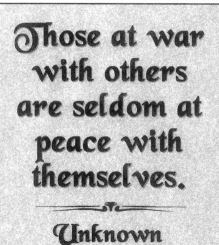

Those at war
with others
are seldom at
peace with
themselves.

Unknown

Chapter 3

5 Reasons Why People May be Difficult with Us

O ne of the reasons that people may be difficult with us is because they have a need to tell us something, and they are afraid that we won't listen. This isn't hard to understand given that, at one time or another, most of us have probably been in this position where we had something important that we wanted to tell someone, but for whatever reason they wouldn't listen. Do you remember how frustrating this was, and how we often became more and more insistent (difficult) trying to get the person to hear us? So do they!

The challenge, therefore, is to respond in a way

that doesn't make them more frustrated and that allows them to tell us what's important to them. This is vital for two reasons: (a) Until they tell us what is on their mind, they will not be open to listening to us, and (b) When they are telling us what is important to them, they are actually giving us *the "key" to their cooperation!*

Unfortunately, many people think the way to deal with difficult people is to let them vent, and when they have run out of steam, *then* you tell them what you want them to know. One problem with this tactic is that it often frustrates the difficult person even more because they don't feel they are being taken seriously. More importantly, however, this technique ignores one of your most valuable sources of information (if your goal is to resolve the conflict), the "difficult person's perspective," *or what's important to them.* Why is this so important? Because, in order to motivate someone to hear what you have to say as valuable, you must frame your communication in a way that includes what's important to them. Where can we find this valuable information? It's often contained *in their "venting".*

So what can we do, especially when we find ourselves caught in the *Cycle of Conflict*? Well, rather than continue to feed the cycle, I'm going to suggest that we stop, set our ideas or agenda aside, and ask a magic question that has the potential to stop any conflict you will find yourself in *for the rest of your life!* Let me demonstrate. Imagine you are in an argument with someone. They are saying this and you are saying that, however, as you become aware of the futility of the situation, rather than continuing to argue, you stop, and ask, "Okay, what is it that you want me to know about this?" or "What's really important to you here?" Think back to some disagreement where you were one of the parties involved in the conflict. Can you see how some form of this question would have interrupted the cycle?

One of the reasons that this question is so powerful is that it's unexpected. Often, it will take the other person by surprise, and have them stop and focus on what they really want you to know, versus continue to slam your position. That's the good news. The bad news is that this element of surprise can also raise their suspicions. Your sudden change in demeanor may have them wondering what you are up to. In fact, they may think you have read some book on "Dealing With Difficult People", and this is some sort of psychological trick!

Therefore, after you have asked the question, rather than assume that you have heard everything that is important to them, I would encourage you to ask again, "Is there anything more?" At this point, they may begin to believe that you are truly interested in their perspective, and tell you a little more about the problem. However, they still may not be telling you everything, and getting all of the information is essential to creating a powerful solution. Therefore, I'm going to suggest that you ask a third time. "Is that all?" Is there anything else?" You really have nothing to lose by asking again, however, if indeed they have not told you the whole story initially, your asking again will often uncover information that could be vital in your attempt to resolve the conflict. Information that you might have been missed had you stopped with the first or second question.

Then, *listen*! But not just for them to run out of steam. Listen for the "key" to their cooperation, what they are concerned about, or what's important to them, *and* listen in a way that convinces them that you have really heard and understood what they said. How can we do that?

Listen in a way that would allow you to paraphrase back what you heard. This seems simple, and yet if you have ever attempted this type of communication, you know that it is actually quite challenging. The closest most of us have come to listening in this intense manner is when we were lost and asking for directions. Here, we took care not to miss a word because we knew the information was important, and even essential for us to get where we wanted to go. I am going to suggest that the same is true when dealing with a difficult person.

In other words, if our goal (where we want to go) is to resolve the conflict in a way that results in their hearing what we have to say, then we must first be willing to model this perspective and listen in a way that not only allows them to tell us what is important to them, but also demonstrates that we are invested in both hearing and understanding what they are saying.

The reason that this is so hard for most of us is

that, often, when we are pretending to be listening, what we're really doing is preparing our response, or thinking about other things. If we want to become truly influential in our interactions with others, however, we must be willing to set our agenda aside, and deal with their need to tell us something, by truly listening to what they have to say, and then checking to see if we heard them correctly. We might say something like, "Let me make sure I'm understanding you correctly. You said _____. Is that right?" The value of asking this last question is that regardless of their answer, we receive very valuable information.

For instance, if they say, "No, that's not what I said (or meant)", then we know we missed something, and because we know that they will not be in a position to hear us until they feel heard and understood by us, we need to find out what we missed. Plus, what we missed might be the "key to their cooperation" and, thus, we want to make sure we hear this as valuable information. If, on the other hand, they answer "yes" to the question, "Is that right?", then we know that we have indeed heard them correctly, and can continue, confident that we are working from facts versus our assumptions.

So we begin by listening to what they need to tell us, paraphrasing what we heard, and checking for accuracy. Great beginning! However, rather than immediately reaching for our ideas and beginning to tell them what we think, let's make sure we have dealt with all the reasons why people might be difficult with us, or resist hearing what we have to say.

Another reason that people are difficult is that they are often afraid that we don't understand the seriousness of the problem, and/or that we see their emotions and behavior as just "overreacting". They not only believe that their problem is a "serious" one, they further believe that they have a "right" to be upset about it, and they may interpret your *not* being upset as "you don't think their problem is a big deal" or "you just don't care". This is why if you have ever tried to tell someone who is upset to "Just calm down" they generally don't say "Thank you for sharing". In fact, they will probably say something like "Calm down? Don't tell me to calm down!", and become even more upset.

Remember the *Lesson of the Fist* which says - *Whenever we try to force someone to change, they will either resist us or resent us, or both, and as a result, become more motivated to defend their position!*

So, what can we do here? How can we respond in a way that allows them to stop defending the seriousness of their problem and their right to be upset? *Empathize.* I know this can sound like psycho-babble, so hang in there while I explain the concept and why this is important. By "empathize", I mean just saying something as simple as, "I can see how you would be upset by this." Many people have trouble with this concept because they are afraid that saying we understand someone's position (or why they might be upset) means that we agree with them.

The important thing to remember here is that *understanding doesn't necessarily mean agreement!* It just means that, based upon how they see the world (their beliefs about the world and themselves), we can understand how they might be upset.

For example, imagine you are dealing with a person who is upset because he believes that martians are controlling our brain waves. If you were to say, "Oh, give me a break! Martians aren't controlling our brain waves!", he would most likely become very defensive and begin to vigorously defend his position. If on the other hand, you said something like, "I can see how you would be upset by that", it wouldn't mean that you *agree with him*. It would, however, allow him to stop trying to defend his position, or his right to believe what he believes.

Remember, our goal, or what we are trying to accomplish here, is to deal with *all* the reasons that a person might be upset with us so that we can move the conversation toward a solution. If a person believes that we see their behavior and/or emotions as "overreacting", or that they have no reason to feel or think the way they do, then they will likely become *more difficult* as they continue to defend the seriousness of their problem, and their "right" to be upset. This is contrary to what we are trying to accomplish. Instead, we want them to stop defending their position and move toward a solution. Empathizing with them sends the message that we are not going to make them defend their position, or their right to be upset. Our decision to empathize, however, doesn't necessarily mean that we agree with their position or reaction.

Okay, we have begun to defuse the conflict by first listening to what they need to tell us, while learning what's important to them. And, now we have empathized with them so they know that we understand the seriousness of their problem, and they no longer need to defend their position. Now do we reach for our ideas and give them our solution? Well, we could, and if you can see that they have become receptive to your opinion, and are clearly wanting to know what you think, then great! However, this can be risky because there are several more reasons why people are resistant to hearing our solutions. So, just in case this is one of the really difficult people, let's cover all the potential blocks to their hearing your position as valuable.

Often, just listening and even empathizing isn't enough to deal with a person's resistance. They may have some specific ideas about how to solve their problem, and may be very invested in you hearing their solutions. If somehow they get the message that you aren't interested in their ideas, they may think, "Well, why should I care about your ideas, if you don't care about mine?"

Here, you can once again use the power of the receptive position and *ask some questions* that can be very helpful in dealing with their resistance. For example, after you listened to their description of the problem, and empathized with the fact that they are upset, you could ask, "What are your ideas about solving this problem?", or "What would be a solution that you would be satisfied with?"

Often, we are reluctant to ask questions such as these because they are afraid that the "difficult" person will "ask for the moon" or something that we can't deliver. I'm going to suggest that, while this sometimes might be the case, asking is still a good idea. Here's why. Asking them for their ideas does at least two things that could be very helpful in resolving the conflict. First, it brings the discussion into the present.

Often, disagreements are based upon who said what, or did what, in the past. This is almost always an unwinnable argument, because they will remember one thing while you remember another. Asking about potential solutions moves the discussion from the past (the problem) to the present, and lays a foundation for moving toward a solution.

Second, when you ask them for their input, you not only demonstrate a willingness to hear and understand their point of view (remember that's what you want them to do with you!), you learn more about the "key" to their cooperation or what's important to them. This is something that we touched on during the discussion on listening, however, I believe that it is so important, it deserves to be mentioned again. In fact, I'm going to suggest that the most critical component in resolving conflict, or dealing with difficult people, is our ability to tap into their internal motivation to hear what we have to say as valuable, and move toward a solution.

In order to do this, we must know what's important to them. Without this information, when it comes time for us to move to the active role and offer solutions, we may find ourselves caught in yet another *Cycle of Conflict*. Instead, when we can learn what's important to them (or what they are concerned about or afraid of), we can then begin to craft a solution that has a high potential of being heard and accepted, because it contains some of *their* ideas and objectives as well as our own.

"Great," you may be saying, "But what if they *do* "ask for the moon" or want something that I can't give them? Doesn't the fact that I just asked them what they want make them even *more* upset when I don't deliver?" Interestingly enough, not necessarily. Remember the reasons we have already discussed as to why people are difficult to begin with, (a) they have something they need to tell us, (b) they are afraid that we aren't taking their problem seriously, and(c) they don't believe that we value their input or ideas. If, after hearing their problem, we immediately begin to tell them why we can't help, they are likely to argue with us because they don't believe that we truly understand the content, or the gravity of the situation.

However, when we sincerely *listen* (so that we could paraphrase what they said back, if necessary), *empathize* so that they no longer have to defend their right to be upset, and *ask* them for their ideas (all receptive skills), we have successfully dealt with many of their initial concerns. They now know that we have at least some understanding of the problem. Then, if we are truly unable to give them what they want in terms of a solution, they will be much more likely to accept this, even though they may not like it.

Interestingly enough, people can tolerate disagreement if they believe that you truly understand their position. What they can't tolerate is being misunderstood, because they believe that if you truly understood, you would agree with them. The receptive skills of *listening*, *empathizing* and *asking* are designed to both understand what's important to them (the key to their cooperation), and have them feel understood so their fear that "you don't understand" is no longer a barrier to their listening to you.

Okay, what's next? Well, the good news is that having used the receptive position to deal with many of the "difficult" person's reasons for being difficult, we are now in a position to address one of the last barriers to problem-solving. They're afraid that we aren't going to address the problem, or that if we win, they lose.

Here is where we begin to move from the receptive position to a more active one and begin to suggest solutions. The difference in proposing solutions here versus at the beginning of the dialogue is that, based upon our willingness to hear and understand their concerns, chances are they will now be much more open to hearing and understanding us. In my seminars, I use the yellow and blue water to demonstrate this by pointing out that as we continue to *listen, empathize,* and *ask,* blending the receptive and the active, (pouring the water back and forth into each cup) the "color" of the interaction changes from yellow and blue (us versus them), to green. This symbolizes how as we hear, understand, and partner with them in moving toward a solution, the "conflict" becomes a problem-solving session, and we begin to combine our two perspectives to reach a common solution.

Why am I suggesting that, whenever possible, we reach a *mutually-agreeable* solution, versus simply "our" solution? Several reasons. First, as we have discussed, they are going to be more likely to listen to, and support a solution that includes some of their goals or objectives. This is where our ability to listen for the key to their cooperation pays off. If, in proposing a solution, we blend what's important to them with what's important to us, they will be more likely to see this solution as feasible, or at least agree to give it a try.

Second, believe it or not, they may have some ideas that *haven't occurred to us!* Taking these ideas into consideration could result in a solution that is *even better than ours!* For many of us, this is hard to imagine. We pride ourselves in coming up with the most effective solutions, and often, find ourselves defending these positions versus listening for ideas that might be better.

Unfortunately, when we do this, we shut off access to a potentially invaluable problem-solving resource: "them" and their ideas. While it is certainly true that sometimes difficult people don't know what they are talking about, often they can offer some valuable insights into potential solutions.

If we are willing to ask them about their ideas, we might find that by combining our ideas with theirs, we not only improve the likelihood that our solutions will be heard, we might discover that these combined perspectives produce a more effective solution. Third, by including their ideas with ours, we lay a foundation for future problem-solving experiences with this person in case this solution doesn't work, or another problem is encountered.

There are several concepts to keep in mind as we begin to take the active position and solve the problem. First, we must determine if this is the best time to offer a solution. Even the "right" solution offered at the wrong time becomes the "wrong" solution. Again, the question is whether the person is open to hearing your ideas.

Often, the difficult person is just too upset to consider *any* solution. If so, postponing the discussion for a few hours, or even a few days, can make a difference, in that it gives the person who is upset (and us) the opportunity to calm down. The thing to remember here is that if you do suggest that the discussion be postponed, make sure to set a time to get back together and solve the problem. Otherwise the person might be concerned that you are just trying to sweep the problem under the rug.

Another important consideration in offering solutions is *how* you begin to frame or state your ideas. For example, many people have learned the importance of acknowledging another's position, and they might say something like: "Yeah, I see what you're saying, *BUT* . . . . " The problem with this phrase is that the word "BUT" almost always negates anything that comes before it, and decreases the likelihood that people will be open to what you say next. It's like going up to someone in your family and saying, "You know, I really love you, *BUT* . . . . ." Most people will immediately become defensive, or on guard in response to a sentence such as this.

Interestingly enough, you can change one little word, and have a tremendous impact on how your ideas are received. For example, you might say something like, "Yeah, I see what you're saying, AND, I have some thoughts about that, as well". The use of the word "and" versus "but" improves the chances that they will be open to hearing your perspective, because it doesn't negate theirs. In addition, it creates the possibility for a "both-and" versus an "either-or" solution.

"Either-or" solutions often create a "winner" and a "loser". The loser then becomes the "ambassador of doom" that we discussed earlier who is now very motivated to go and spread negative "PR" about us and our organization. "Both-and" solutions, however, draw upon the perspectives of all concerned and combine them, rather than choosing one over the other. Not only does this avoid the creation of an "ambassador of doom," it has the potential to create solutions everybody can support.

Now, at this point, there may be a little (or not so little) voice in the back of your mind thinking, "This will never work". In fact, you may even have one especially difficult person in mind, and as you imagine going through the model with him or her, you may be having a hard time imagining them responding in a positive way.

This concern is probably based upon experiences in your past where just listening to, or "being nice" to a difficult person didn't work. Let me suggest two things: 1) The tools and skills that we have been discussing aren't about just "being nice" and hoping that the difficult person will change. They are about you becoming more powerful and influential in the interaction by dealing directly with the "drivers" of their difficult behavior. 2) If you really want to become more effective with the people in your life, remember the Albert Einstein quote: *"Problems cannot be solved at the same level of awareness that created them."*

In other words, if you make your decisions about what you believe is possible in the present and future, based solely upon what you have experienced in the past, you will be limiting what you can do, to what you've done. Remember the power of our beliefs! They determine how we interpret situations, and what we see as possible in the future. This determines how we feel and respond, and ultimately, our experience of life.

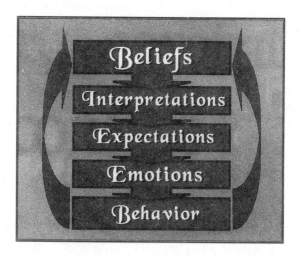

Henry Ford, in speaking to the power of our beliefs, said, "Whether you believe you can or you can't, you're right!" Athletes have discovered the importance of believing in their ability to perform, and even spend significant amounts of time imagining, or picturing themselves accomplishing their goals.

Carl Lewis, Michael Powell and Ivan Pedroso imagine themselves breaking the record over and over again before they actually make the jump. It's almost as if they must take a leap of faith in their mind (seeing themselves jumping over 29 ft.) before they can accomplish this leap in real life. (The world record for the long jump at the writing of this book is 29 feet, 4 and 3/4 inches, held by Ivan Pedroso)

In dealing with difficult people, the problem for most of us is that we have never seen a model, such as the one suggested in this book, used effectively. For example, think back to when there was a conflict within your family, either between you and your siblings, or you and your parents. Did your family members first turn to you and listen to your perspective, and check whether or not they have heard you correctly? Did they, then, work to see the situation from your point of view, and ask you what ideas you have to solve the problem? Probably not. In fact, they probably tried to deal with the conflict in a very "active" manner by insisting that you change whatever they saw as your "problematic" behavior.

Now, I'm not saying that our inability to deal with conflict is "our parent's fault". I'm just suggesting that the *Listen, Empathize, Ask, Problem-solve* model is probably an unfamiliar (or unfamilial) one. Therefore, just like Mike Powell and Carl Lewis must make a leap of faith in their mind, and imagine themselves breaking the long jump record before each attempt, we too, may need to take a L.E.A.P. of faith (Listen,

Empathize, Ask, Problem solve), and be willing to believe in the process in order to learn how to use it effectively.

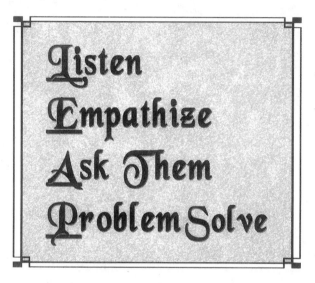

Listen
Empathize
Ask Them
Problem Solve

Now, it's also important to acknowledge that Mike Powell, Carl Lewis, and Ivan Pedroso didn't jump 29 feet, 4 and 3/4 inches the first time they tried. They started off with shorter jumps and worked their way up. Therefore, I'm not recommending that you go out and locate the *most difficult person you can find* to practice on. It's actually better to start with some "annoying" people and work your way up.

Why do we need a model to help us deal with conflict more effectively? Because, what most of us do when someone brings us a problem is immediately begin to problem-solve. This isn't always bad, in fact, sometimes this is exactly what is called for. I am going to suggest, however, that in a situation where conflict exists, or the person or persons we are dealing with are resistant to hearing our point of view, this "problem solving first" approach doesn't work. In fact, what can happen is that our presenting solutions before they are ready to hear them can become a futile "plea" for their attention and cooperation.

Problem Solve
Listen
Empathize
Ask Them

I suggest that as we learn to work with the L.E.A.P. model, where problem solving is the *last* step, we can become more effective in dealing with conflict and actually tap into the difficult person's internal motivation to hear our ideas as valuable information. Because, with the L.E.A.P. model, by the time we begin to offer solutions, we will have dealt with many, if not all, of their reasons for resisting .

The important thing to remember here is that if we encounter resistance during any part of the model, it means that either they still have something that they need to tell us, or that we have missed important information. In either case, it would be to our advantage to go back to "listening" and begin again. Now, I know what many of you may be thinking, "I don't have time to spend all day listening to difficult people! I've got better things to do!" While I can certainly understand this reluctance, I am going to suggest that if you are choosing between the *Cycle of Conflict* and the L.E.A.P. model, getting caught in the *Cycle of Conflict* is far more time-consuming *and* emotionally draining!

THE CYCLE OF CONFLICT

The truth is, once you become skilled in the L.E.A.P. model, you can move through it with most people in about a minute. Now, I'll admit, there are people out there who are more challenging than others in this respect. They seem committed to keeping you from getting a word in edge-wise, and keep talking on and on, going from one tangent to another. What can we do with these people?

First we must be sure that what they are saying is either repetitive (they've said the same thing several times over), or not germane to the topic. In other words, we must be careful not to label their talking as useless gibberish just because it is not what we want to hear. It may actually be good information about what's important to them, or representative of their need to tell us something.

If, however, you have truly determined that what they are saying is not valuable information, there is a way you can interrupt them, and begin to refocus the discussion. I know this is hard to imagine, because it seems that most difficult people will not let you interrupt them for any reason! That's probably because they are afraid that you are just going to tell them they are wrong, and that's not something they are wanting to hear.

In my experience, however, they *will* allow you to interrupt them for one reason... if they really believe that you are sincerely wanting to hear and understand their perspective. For example, you can often be successful in jumping into the middle of their tirade if you say something like, "I'm sorry, I can tell this is important information, and I just want to make sure I've understood you so far. Are you saying_____? Did I get it right?" Again, whether they say "yes" or "no" at this point is good information, and you have refocused the conversation so that they see you as someone who at least wants to understand them versus just argue with them.

Okay, we have talked about many of the reasons why people may be difficult with us or resistant to hearing what we have to say, however, there is one more reason that we have yet to discuss and this one might be the most important. They're afraid that we are going to blame or criticize them.

This is especially true with kids, but also applies to people in general. Any time anyone believes that you are going to blame or criticize them (whether you actually intend to or not), they will argue with you, and/or resist hearing anything you say.

Here, I would encourage you to adopt a brand new rule that deals very effectively with this fear. I say "brand new" because I created it! I call it the "*You Stupid Idiot*" rule! The "*You Stupid Idiot*" rule says that you should never say anything, in any way, where you could end the sentence with "*You Stupid Idiot*".

For example, "No Madam, there's no way we can do it that way! (*You Stupid Idiot!*)" or, "Sir, if you would just read the manual (contract, agreement, whatever), you would see that what you are asking for is impossible (*You Stupid Idiot!*)"

Now, I know what many of you are thinking, "Oh, great! Now I won't be able to talk for the next three months!" Don't feel alone here, for most of us, this response is an almost automatic reaction to anyone who we feel is not making sense (which for the most part means not agreeing with us).

The important thing to keep in mind is our goal or purpose. We want them to listen to what we have to say and/or give us the information we need. If our tone of voice (or any other nonverbal aspect of our communication) is such that we could easily put "*You Stupid Idiot!*" on the end of the sentence, they will put it there *whether we actually say it or not*, and then react by shutting down or beginning to vigorously defend their position. This will make our goal of effective communication much more difficult, if not impossible to reach. This last step turns the **L.E.A.P.** model (Listen, Empathize, Ask, and Problem solve) into the **L.E.A.P.S.** model where "**S.**" is Speak to them in a way that doesn't put them on the defensive (or remember the "*You Stupid Idiot!*" rule.)

Now, I do want to acknowledge that there are people on the planet that you can L.E.A.P. with all day long and it won't make any difference. I'm going to suggest, however, that even with these people, the L.E.A.P. model is a better choice than any response in the *Cycle of Conflict*.

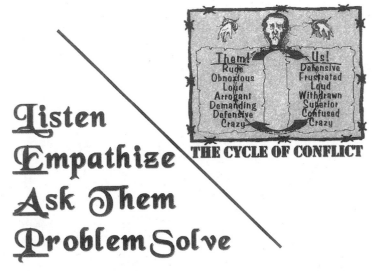

𝕷isten
𝕰mpathize
𝕬sk 𝕿hem
𝕻roblem 𝕾olve

THE CYCLE OF CONFLICT

Why? Well, for one thing, the L.E.A.P. model doesn't give them anything negative to react to, or complain about. If you remember from our earlier discussion, we noticed that if we were to ask "them" (those with whom we find ourselves in conflict), "Who are the difficult people in your lives?", they would say US! In other words, they see *our* reaction as the problem, and use our reaction to justify continuing, or even intensifying their difficult behavior.

When we are able to react by *listening, empathizing, asking,* and then *problem-solving* (remembering the *"You Stupid Idiot!"* rule), we don't give them any "ammunition" to fire back at us, or complain about. I mean, what are they going to say... "They just listened to me too much?" or "They were too interested in what I had to say?"

In my work as a trainer and seminar leader, I have the pleasure of interacting with a wide variety of people and organizations. While good customer service/communication is becoming increasingly important to all of my clients, one group, in particular, has highlighted the importance of following a model, such as L.E.A.P., in their dealings with difficult people. That group is the 9-1-1 dispatchers and telecommunicators who answer the phones twenty-four hours a day all across the nation. Just imagine, you are answering a 9-1-1 emergency call, and the caller is being rude, obnoxious, arrogant, etc., your typical "difficult person." In this case, however, communication (the ability to get information from them, and have them listen to what you have to say) isn't just a good idea, it could be a matter of *life or death*. Plus, *every word you are saying is being recorded* . . . and might wind up on the evening news!

If you can think of the last time you found yourself arguing with a difficult person, and imagine someone was standing there with a video recorder getting the whole thing on tape, you can get some sense of how a professional and purposeful response is critical to this group of under-paid and under-appreciated public servants. They must respond in a manner that not only maximizes the potential that they will get the cooperation they need, they must do this in a way that allows them to maintain a professional demeanor, regardless of how abusive the caller is being. In my work with these public servants, they have told me that the L.E.A.P. model is valuable because it gives them a way to stay engaged with the caller, without falling into the Cycle of Conflict and giving the difficult person something to react to, or complain about.

So, even if the person we are dealing with refuses to cooperate, no matter how much we listen, empathize, etc., the fact that we have responded purposefully and professionally can serve us in that we have kept our cool, and acted in a manner that, if someone were recording our interaction, we would be proud to have that tape played over national TV. Finally, just compare the Cycle of Conflict with the L.E.A.P. model. If your goal is to reduce the amount of stress in your life, which one would you choose?

Okay, so far we have discussed the *Cycle of Conflict,* or how simple disagreements can escalate into a self-perpetuating cycle, and we have learned that when we try to solve the problem from within the cycle by trying to change "them", they become even more difficult *(the Lesson of the Fist)*. We also have discovered how their beliefs about themselves, the world, and us, (as well as, our beliefs about them) can have a powerful effect on their behavior, and on our ability to solve the problem. Further, we have examined the many reasons why people may be difficult with us in the first place, and created a model (L.E.A.P.S.) that not only deals with each reason, but increases the likelihood that they will hear our suggestions in a more favorable light.

So far, so good... but is it possible to stop conflict before it starts? In other words, is there a way to interact with people that allows us to deal with all the tough issues without sweeping them under the rug, *and* without having to go through (and defuse) the Cycle of Conflict? That is exactly what the next section is about.

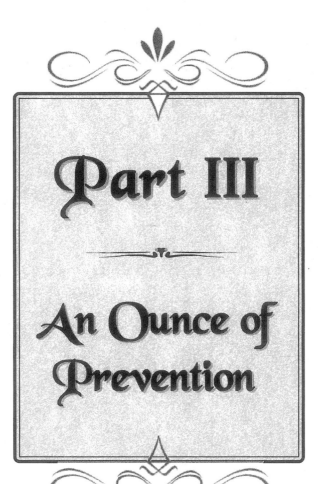

Part III

An Ounce of Prevention

Chapter 4

The Power of Purpose

*A*s we have already discussed, trying to solve the problems associated with conflict from within the *Cycle of Conflict* (i.e., by trying to change "them" first), doesn't work. Further, although dealing with the difficult person's fears and concerns through the L.E.A.P. model is a very effective method for defusing conflict, there is a way of interacting with people that is even more proactive, a way to stop many conflicts before they start. In this third section, I would like to introduce you to this more proactive model so that you may understand and apply the principles and concepts of the model in all of your interactions.

This is actually one of the most valuable aspects of the model we are about to discuss. While the L.E.A.P. model is not designed to be applied to all of our conversations, just those where conflict or resistance is present, this next model could be successfully applied to any and all of your interactions.

In fact, I believe that this is a model that can be applied to any area of your life, from creating a successful career, to becoming a more effective parent, to improving your golf game. For those of you who have read my first book, *All Stressed Up & Nowhere To Go!*, you may remember how this model was applied to dealing with stress. In any case, needless to say that this is a model that is designed to help you become more powerful and influential in all areas of your life. Here we are going to apply it to interacting successfully with others, regardless of the circumstances.

The first step in applying this powerful method to our interactions with others is becoming very clear about *our purpose*. This may sound simple, however, it actually consists of several sub-steps that often require some thought and planning. First, we must become clear about what we want to accomplish, or what is our ultimate goal with this individual or group?

For example, we may want to establish a relationship with this person that makes future interactions more productive, or, we may want them to become an "ambassador of good will", or someone that speaks well of us and/or our organization to others. In addition, as we have discussed earlier, our goal may be as simple as good communication, i.e., we want them to hear what we have to say, and we may need them to give us information from time to time. Whatever you want to accomplish, just be sure to have that goal firmly in mind *before* you begin the interaction.

By the way, in creating this purpose, it is important to remember that for you to be successful, your end result, or what you are wanting to accomplish, must be beneficial to all concerned, otherwise they will just see you as someone who is trying to manipulate them, and resist you even more. Therefore, one way to ensure that your goal or purpose meets that criterion is to imagine saying it to "them" before you begin.

The second part of creating a powerful purpose is becoming clear about *how* we would be dealing with this person (what we would be thinking, feeling and doing) if we were responding to them "on purpose". If you look at *our* part of the *Cycle of Conflict* (our reactions), I don't believe any of us would sat that we react that way "on purpose". In other words, I don't think we would say, "I know, when I am dealing with a loud, obnoxious, and angry person, I am going to feel frustrated, anxious and defensive! Yeah, that's a good idea!"

Now, remember, I'm not questioning whether you "should" or "shouldn't" react this way, but instead, is this response congruent with your purpose? This means not only congruent with what you want to accomplish, but more importantly, *how* you want to accomplish it, or how you would be interacting with this person if you were responding to them deliberately, intentionally, or "on purpose".

I say "more importantly" because I believe that creating a vision of this purposeful, or more deliberate way of responding, is critical to our success with people. In other words, the clearer we are about "who we want to be" in relation to this person, or the qualities that we want to practice in an interaction with them, the higher the likelihood that our interactions will be congruent with our purpose and produce the results we want.

Another way of getting at this somewhat elusive concept is to imagine the person, or type of people, with whom we are wanting to be successful, and ask ourselves, "What is my highest purpose with this person or group?" and then, "If I were interacting with them in a way that is congruent with my highest purpose, what qualities, or characteristics, would I be demonstrating?" These types of questions can often be very powerful when we are thinking of our family and / or those that we hold in high regard.

In fact, starting with those closest to you can be a very good beginning point (even though it is not necessarily easy) because not only are you more likely to have thoughts about your "highest" purpose when you think of your family, but you will also be implementing this more deliberate way of being with the people who are most important to you.

Now, this doesn't mean that we must become purposeful with our family *before* we can respond in a purposeful way with others. In fact, for many of us, our family may be one of the more challenging places to practice living (or responding) "on purpose".

However, I think we can all agree that given the potential upside of being purposeful with our family, it is worth the effort. Plus, as we have discussed, asking the questions pertaining to "purpose" with our family in mind can help us become clear about how we want to be with others.

The challenge here (as it is whenever we want to change *any* aspect of our life) is not to look to the problem (or the pain of the problem) as motivation to change, or as the place to find a solution. As I discussed at some length in *All Stressed Up & Nowhere To Go!*, when we hold an image of the problem and all the "problems-around-the-problem", we often find ourselves trying to solve problems at the same level of awareness that created them (remember Albert Einstein's admonition?).

If we can, instead, become clear about what we are trying to accomplish (our purpose) and how we want to go about accomplishing this purpose (the qualities and characteristics we want to bring to the interaction), we will be focusing on what we want (versus what we don't want), and creating an image of the solution. It is my belief, that we will then be approaching problems and creating solutions at a higher, more purposeful level of awareness.

The end result will be either we are more successful, or we are not. However, even if we are not as successful as we would have liked, we can use our new awareness to change what didn't work. In other words, when we are living "on purpose", or being clear about the impact we wish to have on an interaction, as well as, the characteristics we want to practice, even if we are unsuccessful we can benefit from the experience. This is because we will have a higher level of awareness of what we did, why we did it, and how it worked. This puts us in a very powerful position to effect change, with ourselves and others.

We can even imagine that we have hired this difficult person to be just the way they are so that we can practice responding to them in a more purposeful manner. The good news is that they are actually doing us a great favor by giving us someone to practice with, and we don't have to pay them!

Now, for some of you, this idea may be too far-fetched! In fact, I can just hear some of you saying, "Okay, Bill, now you have crossed the line. I was with you up until this last sentence, but if you think I am going to *pay* people to be difficult with me, or be *happy* that they are being obnoxious, you're out of your mind!%#@!"

This is understandable ... *AND* ... let me ask you this question. Do you think that you will ever encounter another "difficult" person in your lifetime? Well, how much would it be worth to you to be *immune* from his/her "difficult" behavior, or be able to interact with them without taking on their "stuff"?

You see, our current reaction to these people is a "practiced" response. That's why very few of us look at our reactions in the *Cycle of Conflict* and say, "Whoa, this is a brand new experience. . . never done this before!" For most of us, this is a familiar response. We just haven't been aware that we have been practicing.

THE CYCLE OF CONFLICT

So, given that we will always be practicing something (either the *Cycle of Conflict* or responding "on purpose"), and, given that the more we practice anything, the more automatic it becomes, I'm going to suggest that we look for opportunities to practice responding on purpose and even be grateful when these opportunities come along. The more skilled we become at living and responding "on purpose", the more influence we will have in our interactions with others, and our experience of life.

**Happiness is not a reward –
it is a consequence.
Suffering
is not a punishment
– it is a result**

Robert Green Ingersoll

Chapter 5

ᗩhe ᑭower of Our ᑭast

*W*hy don't we interact in this more purposeful way naturally? Why do we find ourselves responding in ways that seems so incongruent with our purpose? Two words... our past. When I say "our past", I am referring to the habits, beliefs, and/or learned responses that have become part of the way we habitually respond to others. Further, I'm suggesting that we pay special attention to those responses and/or patterns of interaction, especially those that are incongruent with our purpose.

Notice, I didn't say those habitual responses that are "good, bad, right, or wrong". That's because

I don't believe that these labels really serve us in our attempt to raise our level of awareness about what is driving our reactions. In fact, I believe that the need to defend, or condemn these beliefs, or ways of interacting with others as "right" or "wrong" is one of the drivers of the *Cycle of Conflict*. Further, I'm not even saying that everything that we learned in our past is "bad", or needs changing.

For example, as I mentioned in my first book, *All Stressed Up & Nowhere To Go!*, I grew up in an A.A. home. My father was a recovering alcoholic, and very involved in the program of Alcoholics Anonymous. I grew up attending A.A. meetings with my parents, and watching them (Mom and Dad) support others in making changes in their lives.

There are many things I learned as a result of growing up in this type of environment that serve me well today as a speaker and counselor. These included the ability to speak in front of others and support others in taking charge of their life. It also must be said, however that not all of the ways of responding I learned as a child are habits and behavior patterns that I want to continue to practice and pass down to my children.

I'm going to assume that you are the same way, i.e., some of the habits and or ways of responding that you learned as a child serve you, and some do not. My goal is not to judge these responses as right or wrong. My goal is to help you become aware of how and why you react to people and/or conflict, so that you can choose to either continue this behavior, or change it.

So how does one begin this process of deciding what to keep, and what to change? Well, first, we might want to revisit the beliefs model to remind us of how powerful our beliefs are in creating these responses.

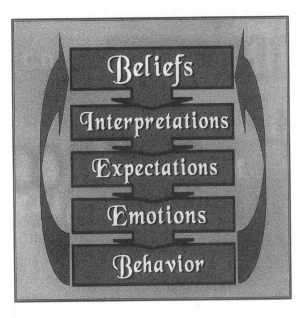

The challenge is that many of these powerful beliefs, which have such a huge impact on how we react to conflict (and life in general), weren't learned "on purpose", but instead are a reflection of what we observed in our family and/or culture. In other words, often what we believe to be true about ourselves and the world (how we interpret, or give meaning to the situations we encounter, what we expect to-happen next, how we feel, and what we do) are, to some degree, the result of our past experiences. Therefore, if we are to become increasingly influential in how we deal with others, we must also become aware of the influence of this past learning.

Some people call this learned perspective our "comfort zone".

I'm sure you have heard this term in reference to what we know, or are "comfortable" with. However, have you noticed that, often, especially in conflict, this "comfort zone" isn't so comfortable, and yet we still have a hard time changing? In other words, have you ever been in an interaction, discussion, or conflict that really wasn't very "comfortable" at all, but you found yourself hard-pressed to change your response? There is a very interesting quote that applies to this dilemma that says:

> **Sometimes we stay in Hell a long time because we have learned the names of the streets**
>
> **Michael Levine**

What this quote so eloquently describes is how and why we continue to react in ways that really don't work for us. We are familiar with this way of interacting, and, therefore, seem to be stuck in the resulting cycle. Even though, at times, it feels like "hell", at least we know the names of the streets, or how to get around, and what to expect. The truth is, this isn't so representative of what we are comfortable with, or our "comfort zone", as what we know, or our "known zone".

Further, any response outside of the "known zone" is, by definition, "unknown", and we all know how hard it is to embrace the "unknown". This is where having established your purpose (in all the ways discussed in the previous chapter) can be valuable because, once you have become aware of how you are responding to situations and/or people (or how you are likely to respond), you can then ask yourself, "Are these responses congruent with my purpose?" Meaning, are they helping me achieve the results I want, and are they congruent with the qualities and characteristics that I would be demonstrating if I were responding *on purpose*?" Our purpose then becomes the "known", and we can use this as the criteria for all of our decisions about which beliefs, emotions, and behaviors to keep, and which to change.

Again, we don't even have to be worried about making the "right" choice, (for we all know that there will be times when we won't know what the "right choice" is until we make it). The fact is that when we are choosing "on purpose", we will be clearer about which decisions lead to which results (rather than being confused about what happened and why). If our choices don't produce the results we want, we can then use this clarity to choose again, and in doing so, continue to refine the process of aligning our decisions with our purpose.

The key is to always strive to be aware of two things, (1) what is our purpose and (2) what old, habitual ways of thinking and responding are likely to get in the way of us responding "on purpose?"

These first two concepts then become the "what" of the model. What we want (our purpose), and what we don't want (old, less-than-purposeful, habitual responses). The next three steps in the model outline the "how", or how we can use our awareness to avoid the *Cycle of Conflict*, and become more influential in our interactions with others and our experience of life.

Live so that when
your children think
of fairness, caring,
and integrity, they
think of you.

H. Jackson Brown

Chapter 6

Conflict and The Wisdom of Serenity

*A*s I have mentioned, many of my beliefs that are congruent with my purpose came from my growing up in an A.A. environment. As a child I spent many evenings playing in, and around, the A.A. meeting halls of east Texas. When I became old enough to read, I began to notice all the "sayings" that adorned the walls of these meeting rooms. "Let go and let God... One day at a time"... very wise sayings that still serve me today. My favorite, however, became the Serenity Prayer which, of course, says, "God grant me the serenity to accept the things I cannot change, the courage to change the things I can, and the wisdom to know the difference."

What does this have to do with conflict and dealing with difficult people? Well, what if this prayer describes the "how", or the process of dealing with people "on purpose". For example, remember the *Lesson of the Fist* which said that whenever we try to force another to change, they will resist us even more? Well, notice what is asked for first in the Serenity Prayer..."God grant me (first) the serenity to accept the things I cannot change". *What if the necessary first step in dealing with difficult people or conflict is to stop trying to change the other person*? Further, what if the necessary precursor to this acceptance is "serenity"? Doesn't this make sense?

In other words, can you imagine how we might react differently to difficult people if, before we spoke, we were able to tap into a sense of serenity, and recognize that, by trying to change them first, we will only escalate the conflict? We could then move to what is asked for in the second part of the prayer, having the "courage to change the things we can". For the most part, this would be our old, habitual reactions to them which, by the way, *will* take courage for us to change.

Further, as we begin to deal with conflict by using "serenity" to avoid trying to change them first, and even accept the fact that, from their point of view, they are understandably upset, we can then summon the courage to change our reaction to a more purposeful, less reactive one. Can you see how this might allow us to determine whether the disagreement we are dealing with can be turned around? In other words, we can develop the "wisdom to know the difference" by practicing the concepts of serenity, acceptance, courage and change... in *that order!*

This emphasis on the concept of "serenity" as a precursor to everything else is also congruent with our earlier discussion of the power of the "receptive" position. Think again of a person skilled in the martial arts, especially a very old and wise master. Can you see how she might begin the process of dealing with conflict by becoming very centered and serene? And from that place of serenity, can you see how she might use the "receptive position" to first move with the energy of an "attacker", and then become more influential in the direction of the interaction? Further, does it make sense that a person who creates this serenity as a precursor to dealing with people, in general, might even avoid many conflicts before they start by being sensitive to another's concerns and dealing with them proactively?

If you remember the first three steps in the L.E.A.P. model, this receptive position refers to the skills of *listening, empathizing,* and *asking.* Each of these skills is designed to gather important information, and at the same time move the interaction toward a successful solution. This is why I call this third step in the process the *Wisdom of Serenity* for it alludes to the power of serenity to help us diffuse the *Cycle of Conflict,* rather than escalate it, and even stop many conflicts before they start.

How one creates this serenity is a very individual preference. Some people pray, others meditate, others listen to music, practice yoga, garden, golf, run, walk, or even play with their pets or their children.

In my first book, *All Stressed Up & Nowhere To Go!*, I describe a model that is designed to help us regain control, and create a moment of clarity and serenity by actually changing the chemical make up of our body (naturally). The five steps in this model not only spell "B.R.A.I.N.", but they are also designed to help us affect the chemicals being produced by our brain. I also describe how this model can be used prior to our finding ourselves caught in a stressful situation so that we can indeed use the *Wisdom of Serenity* as a precursor to dealing successfully with any and all of life's experiences.

The important thing is that we choose this wisdom "on purpose", and take responsibility for creating this sense of serenity early, and often, each day. Once this choice has been made, we are now in a much more powerful position to make other choices about how we want to deal with people "on purpose", rather than having these choices being made *for* us by our old, habitual beliefs, and response patterns.

Okay, so far we have examined how, and why, conflict can so easily escalate into a vicious cycle. We have discovered the powerful beliefs that underlie this escalation, and how by changing our beliefs we can influence our reaction *without needing to change "difficult people" first!* We have also discussed a model for dealing with many of the difficult person's concerns that may be getting in the way of them hearing us, and how this same model can move the interaction toward a successful solution.

Finally, we have examined the power of dealing with people "on purpose", the old, habitual tendencies or reactions that might get in the way of this more purposeful response, and how to use the *Wisdom of Serenity* as a precursor to accepting what we can't change, and having the courage to change what we can. The next step in the model is designed to go to the very heart of an interaction and examine what actually drives our reaction to others, and their reaction to us.

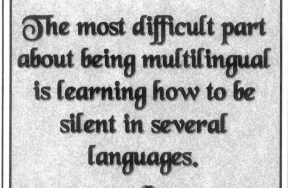

The most difficult part about being multilingual is learning how to be silent in several languages.

Andrew Rombakis, M.D.

Chapter 7

Choosing Your Energy "On Purpose"

*T*his concept of *energy*, which is a critical component to successful interpersonal interactions is somewhat abstract, so let me try to explain it in the clearest terms possible. When I say "energy" I am referring to a driving force even more powerful than our beliefs. In fact, I'm going to suggest that this energy, or force underlies all our beliefs, and even determines the quality (and thus the effect), of our thoughts, emotions, and behaviors, with respect to our interpersonal interactions, and our life in general. The challenge in finding this energy is to first become aware of what is happening now, (i.e. what is driving our collective beliefs and behavior) and determine whether this is congruent with our purpose.

For example, let's go back to some of the material we covered earlier in the book, the reasons why people might be "difficult" with us in the first place, and see if this energy becomes more apparent.

1. THEY HAVE A NEED TO TELL US SOMETHING

2. THEY'RE AFRAID WE DON'T UNDERSTAND

3. THEY'RE AFRAID WE DON'T VALUE THEIR INPUT

4. THEY'RE AFRAID THAT IF WE WIN, THEY LOSE

As we examine these reasons again , can you see how their "fears" are beneath all of these concerns? They are afraid that we won't listen to what they need to tell us, that we don't see their problem as a serious one, that we don't value their input, etc. In fact, I am going to suggest that the entire *"Cycle of Conflict"* is created, maintained, and escalated by fear, both theirs and ours.

In other words, they react the way they do because they're afraid that (fill in the blank with any combination of the reasons discussed earlier), and we react the way we do because we're afraid that (fill in the blank with things like, "They don't like, or respect us, they don't value our opinion, etc., etc.").

THE CYCLE OF CONFLICT

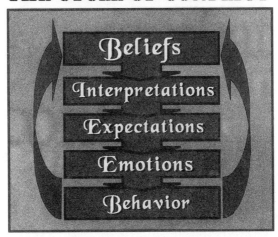

Based upon these fearful beliefs, interpretations, expectations, emotions, and behaviors, they react to us, we react to them, and the ever-escalating cycle of fear goes on and on.

While I *am* suggesting that it is good for us to be *aware* of this fear-based experience, I am *not* suggesting that we be *afraid* of it, and/or that we make changes in how we deal with others based on this fear. That's because I don't believe that fear is the most effective energy for change. In fact, given that we have determined that fear is the energy that underlies and feeds the *Cycle of Conflict*, I'm going to suggest that we use some other energy to address the problem, or more accurately, to create a solution.

What could this energy be? Certainly one could say that awareness would be a better energy than fear with which to build a set of beliefs and responses to people. Awareness of our purpose (what we want to accomplish and how we want to go about it), of the aspects of our past that might interfere with our being purposeful, as well as, awareness of the value of serenity as a precursor to accepting what we can't change and changing what we can. If we believe Albert Einstein's quote that *problems cannot be solved at the same level of awareness that created them*, then choosing a higher level of awareness as the basis for our beliefs and responses would seem to be a very good choice.

In fact, wouldn't it make sense to take Dr. Einstein's concept one step further and say that problems cannot be solved with the same *energy* that created them? Meaning that if fear is the driver of the Cycle of Conflict, maybe we should look to awareness as an energy for change.

Another energy that we might want to combine with awareness could be compassion. Remember the negative effects of resentment (a fear-based energy), it's *like taking poison and waiting for the other person to die,* and the quote from Eric Hoffer that said *compassion is the antitoxin of the soul?*

Remember how our reaction to the difficult person changed when we believed that they had lost their one-year old child in an automobile accident? Remember also, that we are almost always dealing with either an acutely-difficult person (someone like you or I who is just having a bad day) or a chronically-difficult person who sadly lives a life of fear and suspicion.

In either case, wouldn't it be fair to say that compassion would be congruent with our purpose, meaning that the energy of compassion would be supportive in our accomplishing our objective with this person, and doing so in a manner that we would be proud to teach to our children? If we think of the great people in history who we might want to pattern our lives after, isn't one of their more admirable qualities the fact that they were able to be compassionate in some of the most difficult circumstances?

Now, I'm not saying that we *should* feel sorry for difficult people. I'm just saying that the more purposeful we are in choosing the energy that will become the foundation for our responses to people, the more influential we can become in our dealings with others. So the question really becomes, "Which energy do you believe is most congruent with your purpose, fear or something else (like awareness and compassion)?"

Further, for those of you who have a set of spiritual beliefs that serve you well, you might want to include these in the choosing of this foundational energy. I know that this is a very personal decision, and I want you to know that I respect your beliefs in this area. It's just that I have found a simple and effective way to choose the energy that is congruent with *my* purpose, and I want to share that with you so that you can determine if it works for you.

In fact, the only reason that I *wouldn't* share this with you is out of fear that some might see this as too "touchy-feely" and dismiss the book altogether. However, to follow that concern, and leave this part out, would be to make a choice out of fear, and that would be contrary to everything we have discussed thus far. So, here goes.

I have found a very simple question that has helped me choose the energy that I want to guide my thoughts, emotions, and behaviors, every time I have the awareness to ask it. Because I believe that all of our thoughts, emotions, and behaviors *always* stem from one of two energies, *fear* or *love*, when I want to be purposeful in my interactions with others I can always ask myself, "Are my beliefs about this person coming from *love* or *fear*?" This question has never failed to raise my awareness of the energy that is driving my experience, and, therefore, allows me to either continue with, or change this foundational energy, depending on my purpose.

It is important to be clear here that responding to others from "love" doesn't mean that we just lay down, and let them walk all over us, or that we just do whatever they want so that they will be satisfied. And, I'm certainly not suggesting that we allow a person to abuse us in the name of "love". In fact, I'm going to suggest that if we continue to allow ourselves to be walked on, or abused by another, we are actually acting more from fear than love.

Further, I believe that when someone is treating you badly, and especially if this someone is a member of your family, or a person that you are likely to be interacting with over a period of time, the most "loving" thing to do is address this problem with them directly, and if that fails, leave. Because, if nobody ever tells the "difficult person" that the way that they are treating people is driving everybody away, they won't have the information that they may need to change.

Further, if after trying to address the problem in a purposeful way, we continue to stay with a person who is abusing us, the underlying message that we are sending is that this abusive behavior is acceptable. Not a very "loving", or even helpful message.

By the way, I am aware that this aspect of dealing with difficult people (i.e., dealing with an abusive relationship partner) calls for much more discussion than has been allotted here. The reason I have not chosen to go into depth on this subject here is because I believe that (1) we would be well-served by learning to deal with other types of difficult people first, because the better we are at dealing with people in general, the more successful we can be in this generally more-intense situation, and (2) I have plans to write a book completely devoted to the creation and maintenance of successful relationships where I will discuss this aspect of dealing with difficult people much more thoroughly. However, if you are dealing with a difficult or abusive relationship partner now, and can't wait until the next book comes out, remember that being "loving" doesn't mean allowing yourself to be abused, and in fact, one of the most "loving" things you can do for all concerned is address the problem.

The challenge in dealing with a situation like this is to be sure you have tried everything else first, . . . and . . . to be very purposeful in *how* you inform them of what isn't working. The reason I suggest trying everything else first, such as listening to them, trying to understand their position (even if you don't agree with them), asking them for their ideas about a solution, etc. (the L.E.A.P. model) is that "they" may believe that there is a reason for them being upset, and if we begin by telling them what's wrong with them (the *"You Stupid Idiot"* rule), they are not likely to hear our feedback as valuable information. In fact, if you remember the *Lesson of the Fist*, you can see how they may actually become more resistant to what we are wanting them to know.

If, however, our purpose is to give them valuable information about the effect their behavior is having on our relationship, versus strike back, and hurt them like we believe they hurt us, then I believe that this could be done most effectively from a loving perspective.

Now, am I saying that we should just go out and "*luuuv*" all the difficult people on the planet? No. My goal in writing this book is not to tell you what you should and shouldn't do. My goal (or purpose) is to help you become more influential and powerful in your interactions with others by first helping you become more aware of what isn't working, and then become more purposeful in your choices.

In this chapter, what I am suggesting is that the more purposeful we are in choosing the energy that will underlie our beliefs, thoughts, emotions, and behaviors, the more powerful we can be in our interactions with others. I'm also suggesting that the foundational energy behind the problem (or the *Cycle of Conflict*) is fear, and that choosing some other energy to guide your choices would serve you better. Finally, I'm suggesting that a response based upon some combination of awareness, compassion, and love would be more congruent with your purpose (and, therefore, serve you better) than fear.

Love is the productive form of relatedness to others & to oneself. It implies responsibility, care, respect, & knowledge, & the width for the other person to grow and develop. It is the expression of intimacy between two human beings under the conditions of the preservation of each others integrity.

Erich Fromm

Chapter 8

ᴏ̃he Ꝑower of Ꝛesponsibility

*T*he final step in this model (which is designed to not only help you deal with conflict more effectively, but to actually stop many conflicts before they start) is built around the concept of responsibility. For those of you who have read my first book, you may remember that in my early years, I spent most of my life trying to avoid responsibility altogether. I was a musician for the first 15 years of my professional life, and whenever anyone would come up and complain about the band that I was in, I would throw up my hands and say, "Whoa, don't talk to me. I'm just the drummer. I don't make those high level corporate decisions". What I was really trying to say was that, whatever their problem was, it wasn't my fault. That's because I had grown up equating "responsibility" to blame. As an only child, if anything went wrong, it was my fault, and so I tried to make everyone around me more "responsible" than I, so that I wouldn't be blamed.

What I finally came to realize, however, was that the more I gave up my responsibility, the more I forfeited my *ability to respond*. In other words, the more I made other people or situations responsible for my happiness and success (or lack thereof), the less influence I had over my own experience of life. Given that one aspect of my purpose (or what I wanted to accomplish) was to become *more* powerful and influential in how I experienced life, having an "ability to respond" or, an ability to choose my responses to whomever, and whatever, I encountered became a skill I very much wanted to learn.

I am going to suggest that you make a similar choice. In fact, if you really want to become more influential in your dealings with others, and less frustrated by their "difficult" behavior, I am going to suggest that you take *100% responsibility for your "ability to respond"*. What does this mean? Well, it doesn't mean that you are now responsible for the behavior and choices of everyone around you, and it doesn't mean that if some interaction goes bad, you're to blame.

Taking 100% responsibility for your ability to respond just means that you are no longer going to wait for someone, or some situation to change, before you respond in a manner congruent with your purpose. This, of course, means congruent with both *what* you want to accomplish and *how* you want to accomplish it (or the qualities and characteristics you want to practice while in the process of accomplishing your purpose).

It means that your ability to respond, or your ability to choose your responses, and the quality of these responses "on purpose", is so important, that you are willing to be fully accountable for these choices, regardless of the circumstances. It means that you are no longer going to blame others for your responses (emotions, behaviors, etc.) because to do so would give *them* the power to determine *your* experience of life, and my guess is that giving others this kind of power is incongruent with your purpose.

You see, responsibility is power, which means that, the degree to which we are willing to take responsibility for our ability to respond, or to be fully accountable for how we respond to people and situations, is also the degree to which we will have true power in our lives. On the other hand, as long as we hold on to the belief that others have the power to make us respond (think, feel, or behave) in a certain way, (i.e., "He made me so angry!" or "Work just drives me crazy!"), we will be forever at the mercy of the choices and priorities of others. That's why the last step, taking responsibility, is so important.

If we go back to the first chapter of this book and look at "the problem" (the Cycle of Conflict), we can see how the tendency for them to blame us, and us to blame them is a prime component in the creation and maintenance of this vicious cycle.

Them!	Us!
Rude	Defensive
Obnoxious	Frustrated
Loud	Loud
Arrogant	Withdrawn
Demanding	Superior
Defensive	Confused
Crazy	Crazy

THE CYCLE OF CONFLICT

We can also see why taking responsibility for one's responses is a very challenging thing to do. When someone is hurling insults at us and accusing us of all sorts of problematic behavior, it is understandably difficult to respond to this barrage in a "purposeful" manner. However, if we are serious about becoming influential (or powerful) in our interactions with others, stepping back and taking 100% responsibility for the quality of our responses, even in a situation such as this, is exactly what is called for. This is because the only alternative is to continue to blame them for our responses, which only continues to feed the *Cycle of Conflict* and makes "them" the most powerful person(s) in our lives.

There is power in responsibility, whether we accept it, or give it away. There is also power in choosing the energy we want to guide our decisions, emotions, and behaviors.

There's power in honing our ability to stop, and tap into the wisdom of serenity in order to accept what we can't change, and then have the courage to change what we can. There's power in becoming aware of the elements of our past (old habits, tendencies, patterns of responding) that, if left undetected, could sabotage our desire to respond more purposefully to the people and situations in our life. And finally, there's power in acting and reacting "on purpose", or being very clear about what we want to accomplish and what qualities we want to practice while we are achieving this goal.

The operative word here is "power". And, as I have said throughout this book, my goal is to support you in becoming more influential, or powerful, in your interactions with others, as well as, your life in general. That's why I have made the model that we have been discussing in this second section of the book spell POWER, which stands for Purpose, Our past, the Wisdom of Serenity, Energy, and Responsibility.

𝓟urpose
𝓞ur 𝓟ast
𝓦isdom 𝓢er𝑒nity
𝓔nergy
𝓡esponsibility

This acronym is not only designed to help us remember the steps and concepts, but also to "spell out" what it will take to become influential in our interactions, both in terms of how we respond to others, and how they respond to us. Again, if you have read my previous book, or attended any of my seminars, you will recognize this model because I use it in every training, seminar, and workshop that I do. That's because I believe that, regardless of the situation, the more purposeful we are with others, the more we avoid falling into old habits, the more we can use serenity as a precursor to acceptance and change, the more we purposefully choose the energy we want to guide our life, and the more we are willing to take 100% responsibility for our ability to respond, the more successfully we will deal with difficult people, conflict, and all aspects of life. The only challenge with this philosophy is, it's just that, a philosophy. How does it work in real life? That's the question the next section is designed to answer.

Part IV

Real Life

Chapter 9

ᘒhe ᗩrt of ᗝnfluence

1 n this section, I will attempt to give you some concrete examples of how the L.E.A.P. model and the P.O.W.E.R. model can be applied to everyday situations. What we have done to this point is outline the problem (the *Cycle of Conflict*), and two ways to address the problem. The L.E.A.P. model is a more behavioral approach, while the P.O.W.E.R. model is more of a philosophical approach.

Here, I would like to reiterate my belief that two critical components in the success of either of these approaches is sincerity and genuineness. In other words, my goal in presenting these models is not to turn you into a "LEAPing robot" where you are artificially "listening", and then "empathizing" and "asking" as if you are following some script. If a difficult person (or anybody, for that matter), begins to get the sense that you are using some "technique" on them, they will often resist you even more. You must be genuine, which means being who you are, with your own personality, and unique style of communication.

Further, you must be sincere, meaning that you are truly invested in reaching a solution that works for everybody. Neither of these are easy, nor even natural. In fact, some people might say that, "Being who I am is what gets me into trouble in the first place!"

When I am suggesting being genuine, or "who you really are", what I really mean is that you aren't trying to "fake" some way of interacting with people that is foreign to you, or in any way false or phony . . . and . . . I am also suggesting that you choose and emphasize the aspects of your personality that are congruent with your purpose (chapter four). The result of this "genuineness" therefore, is you at your best, or you at your most "purposeful" (which I believe also equates to you at your most "powerful").

In addition to being genuine, the reason I am suggesting that you sincerely pursue a solution that works for everybody, is that when we create outcomes where either we lose or "they" lose, I believe that everybody loses. While *lawyers* might be able to argue against each other in court and then go have a drink afterwards, most people will tell you that the residue left from a win/lose encounter, is counterproductive to any successful collaboration in the future. Add in the stress associated with this type of confrontation, as well as, the potential that the "losing party" will go and spread negative "P.R." about you and/or your organization, and you have all the rationale you need to sincerely pursue a win/win solution.

In addition to being genuine and sincere, there is another distinction we must make in order to apply the L.E.A.P. and P.O.W.E.R. models successfully. That is, we must know the difference between "influence" and "manipulation". Often, when I am presenting this material in a seminar or workshop, one of the participants will ask, "Isn't this just another form of manipulation?" While I can understand the confusion, I am always just a little concerned by this question because I know that if that participant leaves the seminar wanting to be more successful in his/her interpersonal interactions and yet, thinks that the information presented can be used to manipulate others, he or she is doomed to failure. Let me, therefore, make sure that I don't do you the disservice of leaving you with the impression that "influence" and "manipulation" are interchangeable, and, therefore, set you up to fail.

Let's look at how Webster defines the concepts of "influence" versus "manipulation":

Manipulation: to control or play upon by artful, unfair, or insidious means, especially to one's own advantage.

Influence: to affect or alter by indirect or intangible means;

to act upon (as a person or a person's mind or feelings) so as to effect a response.

Can you see the important difference? The definition of "manipulation" contains the words "unfair, insidious" and "to one's own advantage" (versus, for the good of all concerned), while the definition of "influence" just speaks to the concept of effecting a response. This is a good example of how the "energy" we choose to guide our thoughts and behavior can have such a powerful effect on the results of an interaction (chapter seven).

When we are attempting to *manipulate* someone into doing what we want by unfair or insidious means, (a negative energy, i.e., using some psychological model to trick them into agreeing with us), I believe that the other person will sense this, and resist us even more. On the other hand, if our desire is, instead, merely to *influence*, and the other can see that the outcome we are trying to create is beneficial for them, as well as, us (a more positive energy), they are more likely to cooperate. Further, they are also more likely to see subsequent interactions with us in the same light, which increases the potential for more successful outcomes in the future. That's why I'm suggesting that the L.E.A.P. and P.O.W.E.R. models be combined so that you are drawing upon the concepts that you believe will be the most productive and beneficial for all concerned, but are not practicing some "manipulative technique".

The challenge, of course, is how to combine these models in a way that is both natural and effective. While, to a large degree, this will be a different experience for each of you, I am going to attempt to give you some examples of how the models might be used in different situations. Just remember that these examples aren't designed to tell you what you "should do", or how you "should do it". They are simply an attempt to move from a discussion on behavior and philosophy (L.E.A.P. and P.O.W.E.R.), to more of an application-based dialogue. As always, you decide what works for you!

If you would persuade, you must appeal to interest rather than intellect.

Benjamin Franklin

Chapter 10

Dealing with Difficult Clerks

*L*et's start this discussion with the group of people that I find the easiest to deal with: difficult clerks, receptionists, wait staff, etc. Basically, anyone who you need to deal with to get something done, but will probably never encounter again. I believe that these folks are the easiest because, (1) If they are being rude to everybody, it could be that everybody is being rude to them first (say in the example of an airline employee dealing with irate passengers), or (2) They are just having a bad day (or life), and are inciting rudeness in everyone they encounter, but since we will never see them again, we don't need to be concerned about future ramifications with regard to this person. This doesn't mean we don't care whether they cooperate with us. It just means that if, after trying our best to turn the interaction around (applying the L.E.A.P. and P.O.W.E.R. models, etc.), they still are clinging to their rudeness, we can know that we did our best, and maybe even feel some compassion for someone who is obviously living a very sad life.

One of the reasons I find this type of person or situation easiest to deal with is because, by choosing how we want to interact with this person "on purpose", we can have the advantage of surprise, or at least become the exception to the rule. In other words, if, for whatever reason, the difficult person is expecting everyone he or she encounters to be upset, and we respond differently, in that moment of unexpected civility, can lie the opportunity to turn the experience around.

Let's take the airline clerk for example. At one time or another, we have probably all witnessed a scene where some poor clerk is trapped behind a counter trying to explain to a mob of angry passengers why their travel plans have been delayed or canceled. Let's imagine we are in line, and are watching each person before us try to "win through intimidation", and we see the employee become more and more hardened in their responses.

What if, rather than becoming just one more screaming customer, we choose to respond "on purpose"? What might that response look like? Well here, rather than beginning with "listening", we might start instead with "empathizing". We might smile, and say something as simple as, "Rough day?" Chances are that the clerk will be so grateful that we aren't trying to blame him or her for the situation, they may begin to respond to us differently.

After establishing this more purposeful connection, we might then ask them what could be done about our situation. Often, again because we have treated them with empathy and respect, and because everybody else seems to be bent on beating them into submission, they may go out of their way to help us in ways that they wouldn't have done otherwise. We win, *and* they win, because they can feel good about helping a person who treated them well.

Even in the worse case scenario, however, where either the clerk stays in their defensive, belligerent mood, or where nothing can be done, and we are treated just like everybody else, we still win because we have purposefully decided how we want to think, feel, and behave in the interaction, and, therefore, are likely to go away dealing with whatever happens in this same "purposeful" manner. While we might feel a little disappointed that we will be inconvenienced by the situation, we will have tapped into the *Wisdom of Serenity* to accept the things we can't change, chosen the energy we wish to guide our reaction, and taken 100% responsibility for how we experienced it.

In other words, we will have not given that person, or situation, the power to "make us feel" anything, but instead, exerted our own personal power in choosing how we want to respond. Further, rather than finding someone to tell our story to, and, thus, experience the frustration and resentment over and over, we can just allow the interaction to fade from our memory, leaving no "toxic", resentful, residue.

Now, remember, I'm not saying this is how you "should react", or that you have "no right" to become upset in a similar situation. I'm just suggesting that a more purposeful response, such as the one we have discussed, would serve you better, regardless of the outcome, and allow you to be more powerful, or influential, in how you experience life.

Chapter 11

Dealing with Difficult Employers

*U*nlike clerks, receptionists, or others in this category, dealing with a difficult boss or employer can be somewhat more challenging. This is because (1) they have the ability to affect our lives in ways others don't, and (2) we *will* see this person again, and the way we deal with them now will affect future interactions. For both of these reasons, I believe that it would serve us to become very skillful and powerful (versus manipulative) in our experiences with these types of individuals.

Here is where the L.E.A.P. model could be just the thing to call upon because, first, most employers are almost always telling employees what they want them to know. In other words, if your boss is being difficult with you, it might be because they have something they need to tell you, and they're afraid that you won't listen. Here, listening sincerely to what they are saying, and checking for accuracy now and then might convey to your boss that you are really hearing, and understanding what he or she wants you to know. If they really believed this, they might not feel the need to continue to raise their voice or temper to make sure you "get it".

While you are listening to what they have to say, I would also encourage you to listen for the "key to their cooperation" (what's important to them, or what they are concerned about). In this sort of relationship, where the difficult person really *can* influence the quality of your life, finding the "key to their cooperation" is a critical component of success. Now, when I use the term "success", I am not referring to the ability to "fool" your boss into thinking you believe something you don't.

I am speaking of creating a relationship where he or she sees you as a valuable component in the success of the organization (and, thus, his or her success, as well). To do this, you must know what he or she is trying to accomplish, and how you can help make this happen. It would also be advisable to make sure you can understand (or empathize with) their position, feelings, and behavior, even if you don't agree with them.

Remember:
Understanding doesn't necessarily mean agreement!

Further, unless you want them spending their time and energy convincing you that they have a "right" to be difficult and upset, you may want to convey that understanding by saying something like, "I can see that this is very important, what would you like me to do first?" This statement and question combines the "Empathize" and "Ask" steps of the L.E.A.P. model and begins to move the discussion toward a plan of action. It's in the next step (Problem-solving), that you can begin to blend what you know is important to your boss with your suggestions and ideas. (See chapter three)

Having said all this, we must also acknowledge that there are some bosses out there who believe they must treat their employees badly out of fear that the workers will take advantage of them. These are some of the most difficult types of employers to deal with because, often, they're afraid that if they "give in to", or treat an employee with respect, that the employee will not work as hard, or do what they are told. If you have the misfortune to work for a boss like this, as I see it, you really have only three options:

1. Try to convince him or her that you can understand their desire for you to be as productive as possible (the "key" to their cooperation), and you believe that you could be even more productive if they would treat you differently. They will likely find this hard to accept, because the concept of treating people well, and having them become more productive as a result, is probably incongruent with their beliefs. They

may be willing to try, however, if you can tie this experience to some tangible measure of productivity.

2. Just try your best to survive by recognizing that your boss's dysfunctional attitude and behavior is really a manifestation of his or her fears, and you are not going to spend your energy worrying about how those fears might be expressed next. This basically means that you are going to just try to do your job, and let your boss's rants and raves roll off your back. While this is possible, it is by no means easy. Therefore, if you do choose this method of dealing with difficult bosses, give yourself time to become skilled at this benign indifference.

3. Leave. As we have discussed earlier, when one is dealing with a person on a regular basis, and that person has some influence in what happens in your life (such as an employer, or spouse, roommate, etc.) often the best way to rid yourself of the problem is to leave the situation. The challenge is to take some time to examine how you got into that situation in the first place, and make sure that you don't just keep repeating that mistake with a new employer, mate, etc.

Finally, I believe that one of the reasons dealing with difficult employers is so challenging is that, for many of us, having someone telling us what to do, being disrespectful to us, has some deep roots that can be especially uncomfortable. Just think back to what it was like as a child when it seemed like almost everybody was telling you what to do, and this resistance to authority isn't so hard to understand. When we encounter employers today (especially difficult ones) who remind us of this parent/child dynamic, we can often find ourselves reacting in ways that don't serve us.

I believe that the remedy for this tendency to resist authority is to (a) always be self-employed so that the only difficult boss you have to deal with is yourself, or (b) always see yourself as working *with* an organization, rather than *for* it. In other words, rather than see ourselves as someone who is dependent on an organization for our security and welfare where we must "obey" people we don't respect, and submit to being treated disrespectfully out of fear of being fired, I am suggesting that you, instead, see yourself as an independent consultant.

The truth is that you probably bring some very valuable skills and attributes to your work, and chances are your employer is very lucky to have you. Now, seeing your state of employment from this perspective doesn't mean that you snub your boss's authority, or make demands about how he or she "should" treat you (chances are that these snubs or demands will only make the employer more difficult anyway). It means that you see yourself as an important cog in a bigger wheel, and that you work with everybody above and below you, to make the organization successful, because in doing so, *you* become successful as well.

It's really more of a state of mind that has you

cooperating with, and even supporting those in positions of authority, because that is part of what you have agreed to do in taking this job. What you have not agreed to, however, is to be treated with a lack of respect, and so, if this happens (especially on a regular basis), you address it in the ways we have discussed, and if it doesn't change, you leave. As an individual who has valuable skills to offer, you then go in search of an organization that *will* treat you with the respect you deserve.

In doing so, you have actually done a favor for all concerned. Certainly you will feel better given that you have taken yourself out of an abusive situation. In addition, you have sent the message to your disrespectful employer that if they want to keep valuable employees, they may want to re-examine how they are treating them. In this time of tight labor markets, the good news is that more and more employers are discovering the benefits of partnering with their employees, and treating them as members of a team, versus people to be ordered around.

The only caveat here is to be careful that this (leaving because you aren't getting the respect you deserve) isn't happening over, and over, and over. If this is the case, you might want to examine the common denominator in all of these situations. It may be you, and if you continue to blame "them" for your misfortune, you will continue to be powerless to change.

Chapter 12

Dealing with Difficult Employees

I n addition to dealing with stress and difficult people, one of the seminars I am often asked to present is entitled *Training and Keeping Good Employees.* I always begin that seminar with the reminder that this material is about training and keeping GOOD employees, because to spend time and money training and keeping bad employees is not recommended. In fact, to continue to pay an employee to do sub-standard work is not only bad for the organization, I believe that it is a *disservice to the employee.* It's like staying with an abusive partner. The message that is being sent is that their behavior is acceptable (because they are continued to be paid to do it) and, therefore, they have no motivation to change.

I believe that, sometimes, the kindest, most supportive thing an employer can do for an employee who is not doing their job is to let them go. Chances are, if you are the first, or second organization to have fired them for poor performance, they will blame you. However, if you are the ninth or tenth organization to have let them go, they just might begin to do some soul-searching, and recognize that the common denominator in all of these experiences is *them*. This then could result in their re-examining their work habits, and making needed changes. At least by letting them go, you have given them the opportunity to change, versus continuing to pay them to do substandard work.

The challenge, of course, is to know when you have given the employee the chance to correct their mistakes, and to raise the quality of their work to an acceptable level. Here is where the L.E.A.P. and P.O.W.E.R. models can be helpful. For example, often, when we are trying to help an employee raise the quality of their work, they can be resistant to hearing what we say as the valuable information that it is.

There are many reasons why this is the case. For instance, they may have a need to tell us about how "it's not their fault". If we are unwilling to hear this, and/or understand how they might feel this way (Listening and Empathizing, the first two steps of the L.E.A.P. model {chapter three}) they will likely spend most of their energy trying to convince us of the righteousness of their position, or just shut down and tune us out. Again, we don't have to agree with them, just be willing to hear and empathize with how they see the situation.

Another reason employees resist hearing and / or valuing our suggestions is because they don't believe that we value theirs. Here is where the third step in the L.E.A.P. model (Asking them for their ideas) can be helpful. Not only is the employee more likely to support an idea that *they* came up with, but often, given that they know themselves better than anyone else, they will have some excellent ideas about how they could improve their performance.

Of course, the most powerful reason employees don't hear our suggestions for change is that they are afraid that we are going to blame and / or criticize them versus help them improve the quality of their work (and, thus, their chances for success). This is because the employer/ employee relationship can often feel like a parent/ child relationship, where the employee reacts much like a submissive (but resentful) or rebellious child, or adolescent.

Here it is imperative that we remember the "You *Stupid Idiot rule*", and speak to them in a way that doesn't put them on the defensive, or in a way that we couldn't put "*You Stupid Idiot*" on the end of our sentences. This is important because if they hear the unspoken "*You Stupid Idiot*", or believe that we hold them in such low esteem, they will immediately shut down, and any hope of their taking our suggestions to heart will be gone for good.

Hopefully, you can see how the L.E.A.P. model

could be helpful in dealing with a resistant employee. Let's look at the P.O.W.E.R. model. Wouldn't it be reasonable to say that the more purposeful we are as we deal with difficult employees, the more successful we are likely to be? This, of course, refers to our clarity about what we want to accomplish, and most importantly, how we want to accomplish it, (the qualities and characteristics we want to demonstrate while we are accomplishing our purpose). Further, can you see that if we are aware of the habits or tendencies that might keep us from interacting in this more purposeful way, we will be in a better position to avoid slipping back into these old habitual response patterns?

Can you also see how the *Wisdom of Serenity* (the ability to accept what we can't change and then have the courage to change what we can), might help us accept the fact that, even though getting the employee to change is our ultimate goal, we might want to begin by changing how we are interacting with them? Further, given the employee is probably acting out of fear, and that this fear will likely be one of the reasons they will have difficulty hearing us, doesn't it make sense that choosing an energy other than fear to guide our decisions and behavior might be helpful?

And, finally, given that what we really want is for the employee to take more responsibility for the quality of their work, doesn't it make sense that the more we are willing to take 100% responsibility for the quality of our interaction with them, the more we will be modeling the concepts we want them to adopt?

The bottom line is that dealing with difficult employees presents some unique challenges. The good news is that at least with employees, if, despite our best efforts they still refuse to change, we can let them go, and even know that, in so doing, we are giving them very good information about how their behavior may not be serving them. With other people in our lives (like family members), this isn't the case, meaning that we can't just "let them go" and know that it is for the best. What *can* we do? The next chapter is designed to answer that question.

Those who love to be feared and fear to be loved, they themselves are more afraid than anyone.

Saint Francis de Sales

Chapter 13

Dealing with Difficult Family Members

A s we have seen in the previous chapters, different types of "difficult" people require slightly different approaches in terms of how we apply the L.E.A.P. and P.O.W.E.R. models. This is especially true with family members. Further, the "stakes" are generally higher with family members (meaning that everybody has more to lose), and so the intensity of the interactions will probably be greater. Finally, as we have previously discussed, we can't always just fire, or walk away from the members of our family, and so learning to deal with these people can be extremely important.

Unfortunately, one of the challenges of trying to create a way to deal effectively with this category of "difficult people" is that the term "family member" can represent such a wide variety of people and situations. For example, do we deal with distant aunts and uncles the same way we would deal with our significant other? Well, yes and no.

As with all difficult people, there are similarities that are constant regardless of the relationship or the situation. For example, I think we have established that, in general, difficult people are frightened, meaning they're either afraid that we won't listen to them, we don't understand the seriousness of their problem, and/or we don't value their ideas.

Further, they fear if we create a solution, it means that they will lose, or that we are going to blame or criticize them. Again, these fears are likely to be stronger with family members than with others because there is more to lose if something goes wrong. Plus, I think it's also true that most of us have the expectation that our family should be a place of love and acceptance, even a haven from the stress and strife of the "outside world".

Unfortunately, these combined fears and expectations can quickly produce a *Cycle of Conflict* that has the potential to go on for years, if not generations (remember the Hatfields and the McCoys?). There is a quote that speaks to how powerful these familial fears can be, and it says:

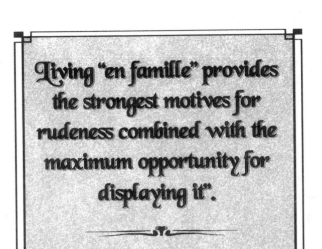

Living "en famille" provides the strongest motives for rudeness combined with the maximum opportunity for displaying it".

Quentin Crisp

This quote also speaks to why we seem to treat members of our "family" in ways we would never even dream of treating a stranger. Needless to say that for all the reasons we have discussed, dealing with conflict within families can be one of our more "difficult" challenges.

That's the bad news. The good news is that while there may be motives for rudeness between family members (as Mr. Crisp has suggested), there are also motives for resolving conflicts that are equally as strong. For example, I think it's fair to say that few, if any of us, want our experiences with our families to be problematic or conflicted. Quite the contrary, I believe that most of us would say that we have a very strong desire for our families to be places of love, trust, and acceptance. Further, because we know that we will likely be interacting with these people for the rest of our lives, we would like this extended relationship to be as harmonious as possible.

Therefore, the challenge in dealing with difficult family members is to remember that under their "difficult" emotions and behaviors lies a desire to "get along," and a strong fear of rejection. I am going to suggest that you deal with a difficult (frightened) family member the same way you would deal with a frightened child who is acting out. Chances are that you wouldn't react to them in a way that made them more frightened, but, instead, you would see through their rude exterior, and interact with them in a way designed to diffuse their fears.

This then would become your purpose (diffusing their fears), and you could then become clear about the qualities and characteristics that you want to embody as you interact with them on purpose. You might also want to be aware of any past habits or ways of responding that might be incongruent with your purpose. Further, you might want to honor the *Wisdom of Serenity* so that you can accept the aspects of the situation that you can't change ("them"), and focus on changing the ones you can.

While dealing with this family member in a more purposeful way, you might become clear about the energy you want to guide your thoughts, emotions, and behaviors, especially given that fear is the underlying energy of the problem. And finally, you might want to take 100% responsibility for your ability to respond, or choose to interact with this person in a way that is congruent with your purpose regardless of how frightened they are, and how that fear might manifest itself in their behavior.

As you interact with them in this more purposeful way, you might also listen more, as well as, empathize so they no longer have to defend their right to be upset, ask them for their suggestions, and then problem-solve by blending their ideas, goals, and motivations (the keys to their cooperation) with yours. In doing all of this, it will, of course, be important to remember the *"You Stupid Idiot"* rule which, as we have discussed, seems to be more of a problem with members of our family than even strangers.

All of this applies except, of course, when you are dealing with a family member who is being physically abusive. Here, as we have discussed, it is important for all concerned that you not send the message that this sort of behavior is acceptable by allowing it to go unaddressed. You can still use the P.O.W.E.R. model to address it, however, by saying something like. "I care for you and our relationship too much to stay and be treated this way. When you are ready to create a relationship based upon our mutual love and respect, then we can discuss how to make this happen" (which, by the way should involve counseling with a qualified family therapist).

In this way, you are establishing your purpose (creating a relationship of love and respect, or none at all), and taking responsibility for stopping the abuse. Again, a gift to all concerned.

As I mentioned earlier, I am aware that this

subject (dealing with difficult family members) really requires much more attention than is given here. However, I plan to write two more books on the subject of creating successful relationships. One will be designed to address the challenges of our most intimate relationships, and the other will be focused on our relationships with our children called: *How To Get Kids To Do What You Want!* I will be discussing this subject much more thoroughly in both of these upcoming books. However, the concepts presented in both the L.E.A.P., and P.O.W.E.R. models, will certainly be part of that discussion.

Chapter 14

Dealing with Difficult Customers

*I*n my work as a trainer and speaker to organizations around the country, one of the most requested seminars from both management and employees alike is Dealing With Difficult Customers. I would venture to guess that the reason this title is so much in demand is because (a) the concept of customer service, or interacting with a customer in a way that keeps them happy, is being recognized as critical to the success of any organization, and (b) the experience of dealing with difficult customers can be one of our most challenging.

The reason this type of interaction is so problematic is that often, we, as the employee, are experiencing two seemingly contradictory impulses. One is to tell this %$#@*&! that they have no right to treat us this way, and the other is to keep the customer happy for the good of us, and our organization.

Often, this dichotomy results in people smiling on the outside while, at the same time, screaming on the inside, all in the name of "good customer service". I'm going to suggest that this is not a very effective solution because of all the reasons discussed in chapter one (we become overly stressed, they go and complain, we carry this tension into our next interaction, etc., etc.)

Instead, let's apply the P.O.W.E.R. and L.E.A.P. models to this situation, and see if they can help. First, of course, we would become clear about our purpose, or the impact we want to have on the interaction. Notice I didn't say focus on what we *should* do, but on the impact that we *want* to have. This is a critical distinction because it moves us from the role of a resentful employee, to that of a purposeful problem-solver who is choosing our responses based upon what we want to accomplish.

We might want to recognize that the difficult customer probably has some information about their problem that they want us to be aware of, but are afraid that we won't really listen. They may be afraid that we won't take their problem seriously, or that we aren't interested in their ideas about how to solve the problem. They may be afraid that if we win, they lose, or that we are unable, or unwilling to create a solution that will be beneficial to them. They may even be afraid that we are going to blame or criticize them, and so are already planning their counter-attack to prove that we are to blame. If you think that your customers might be holding on to any of these fears, you might also see how taking a leap of faith by Listening, Empathizing, Asking, and then Problem solving (chapter three), might be a good way to address these fears while creating a mutually-beneficial solution.

In addition to being clear about your purpose, and using the L.E.A.P. model to accomplish it, you might want to make sure that you aren't falling into any old, habitual response patterns (with respect to how you used to deal with customers that were upset with you) that might be incongruent with your purpose. You might want to call on the *Wisdom of Serenity* to help you push the pause button so that you can deal with the situation without needing the customer to change first.

Further, given that fear is the energy underlying the difficult customer's perspective (i.e., they're afraid that you won't listen, you don't care, etc.), you might want to be sure that you are choosing a different energy to drive your response, one that is congruent with your purpose. And finally, you might want to take 100% responsibility for your ability to respond so that you are being as influential as possible in how you deal with this customer, rather than waiting for them to change first.

I am going to suggest that, to the degree you are willing to master the steps outlined above, you will not only become skilled at dealing successfully with any customer at any time, you will also become more influential in creating your experience of life with anyone you meet. How do you master these steps? That is what the final chapter is designed to address.

Chapter 15

ᎧᎻ Wisdom School

I f you really want to master the ability to deal with any person, at any time, you might want to consider enrolling in a "wisdom school". The concept of a "Wisdom School" is an ancient one. Long ago, schools didn't try to teach knowledge, they taught "wisdom". Further, the teaching techniques were not centered around a classroom, but experiences in everyday life. In fact, there is a quote from Confucius that speaks to the concept of learning by becoming totally involved in the lesson. It says:

Tell me and I will forget,
Show me and I might remember,
But involve me, and I will understand,

Unfortunately today, that concept of learning by immersing oneself in the experience is almost a lost art except to the most skillful of teachers and facilitators. However, let's assume that such an experiential learning laboratory exists. Further, let's assume that you wanted to become more powerful and influential in dealing with difficult people, and so you signed up for this world-famous wisdom school that guaranteed that you would become skilled at dealing with all sorts of problematic people in four weeks. It was very expensive, however this ability was very important to you, and so you paid your fee, and signed up.

First, you would be provided with a day or two of training in listening, empathizing, asking or engaging, problem-solving, and general "purposeful interaction, so that you could integrate the concepts into your own unique style of communication and conflict resolution. Then, for the rest of your stay, you would be provided as many difficult people to practice with as you wished. The types of people and situations that you "encountered" would be especially chosen to match the types of people and situations in your everyday life. Each of these "practice opportunities" would be recorded and you could then review your progress on a daily basis. How do you think you would do? My guess is that you would do very well, because you would be interacting with all of these difficult people "on purpose".

In other words, you would know precisely *why* you were dealing with them and *what* you wanted to practice. Given that anything we practice for twenty-one days in a row becomes a new habit, at the end of your four-week retreat, you would have developed some new habitual ways of dealing with people that would be much more congruent with your purpose.

Well, I've got some good news and some bad news. The bad news is that I'm not aware that a formal program like this actually exists, at any price. The good news is that you can still "enroll" yourself in the program... it's free... it's called "life"!!

In other words, if you wanted to become skilled in dealing effectively with others, regardless of the situation, and you were willing to see each person you encountered as an opportunity to practice, you could create your own "Wisdom School". By practicing responding "on purpose", (Listening, Empathizing, Asking, and then Problem solving), changing any old habits that might be incongruent with your purpose, drawing upon the *Wisdom of Serenity* to help you accept what you can't change (and summoning the courage to change what you can), continuing to choose the energy that supports this more purposeful style of interaction, and finally, taking 100% responsibility for your ability to respond, I believe that you could become much more powerful in your interactions with others, and your experience of life.

This, in a nut shell, has been the purpose of

this book, to help you become more influential and powerful in all of your interpersonal interactions. Again, this is why the final model spells POWER.

ℙurpose
ℚur ℙast
𝕎isdom ˢ𝑒𝑟𝑒𝑛𝑖𝑡𝑦
𝔼nergy
ℝesponsibility

Given that we will always be practicing something, our challenge is now, to become clear about what we want to practice.   In other words, what are the concepts and beliefs that we will trust to guide our future decisions and behaviors with respect to our interactions with others? For example, are we going to continue to point out other's difficult behavior and blame them for our reaction? Are we going to keep throwing up our hands, and lamenting that we are just the victims of all the difficult people in the world? Or, are we willing to take a L.E.A.P. of faith, create our own "wisdom school", and use our future interactions to become skilled at trusting the power of purpose, serenity, awareness and our ability to respond?

The real question is, "Are we going to claim our responsibility and power with respect to our interpersonal interactions, or continue to give our power away to others? My purpose in writing this book has been to support you in claiming this power and influence... the power to deal with difficult people versus them dealing with you... the power to deal with conflict without losing your head... the power to move *from chaos to calm.*

Keynotes, Trainings, & Other Presentations

If you enjoyed the material in this book and believe that it would be valuable for others in your organization, the keynote or training based upon this book is entitled *Dealing with Difficult People!* Dr. Crawford is also known for his ability to impact audiences on several other topics. The most popular of these are listed below:

All Stressed Up & Nowhere To Go!

How to Talk So That People Can Listen

Training and Keeping Good Employees

How To Get Kids To Do What You Want

Contact Dr. Crawford at:
1-888-530-8550
or
www.billcrawfordphd.com

About the Author

Bill Crawford, Ph.D. is a psychologist, organizational consultant, corporate trainer, and professional speaker currently residing with his wife and two children in Houston, Texas. His corporate clients include many of the Fortune 500, as well as, professional associations and a variety of other organizations nation-wide. He holds a Bachelors of Music Education, and both Masters and Doctoral degrees in Counseling Psychology from the University of Houston. He is also the creator and host of two PBS specials entitled *All Stressed Up & Nowhere To Go!* and *From Chaos to Calm: Dealing with Difficult People.* Known for his dynamic, entertaining, and yet practical presentations, Bill blends humor with concrete, "real world" suggestions to support individuals and organizations in reaching their personal and professional goals.

How to Order Additional Books

If you would like to share this information with your family, friends, or members of your organization, you can order copies of Dr. Crawford's books in any quantity. As price per book and shipping costs will vary depending upon the number of copies ordered, please contact us at **www.billcrawfordphd.com** or call **1-888-530-8550** for more information.

Notes

Notes ❧

Notes

Notes

Notes